A Prophetic Minority

Jack Newfield
A PROPHETIC MINORITY

Introduction by **Michael Harrington**

 **THE NEW AMERICAN LIBRARY**

A society is renewed when its humblest
element acquires a value.
—Ignazio Silone

Contents

A Prophetic Minority

Introduction
By Michael Harrington

The young and resurgent radicals of the 1960's—the New Leftists—are, for the most part, the privileged children of the affluent middle class. They are numbered in the thousands, a mere fraction of their generation, only a small percentage even among college students. They are courageous, dedicated, and existential in a way that sometimes borders on the anti-intellectual. So they are rather weak on social and political theory, and they have dismissed most of the veterans (i.e., over thirty years old) of the American movements for social change as irrelevant failures.

Jack Newfield thinks that this handful of radicals constitutes a "prophetic minority" that will stamp its image on these times and eventually affect American history itself. I think Newfield is right.

It is, of course, a commonplace of American history that this society tends to co-opt the ideas of its third-party movements but retains the two-party system with all of its amorphousness and resistance to open ideological conflict. So, one is often told, the immediate demands of the Debsian Socialists of 1912 were carried out by the liberal reform movement of the New Deal (and, more often than not, "carried out on a stretcher," as Norman Thomas likes to remark). But I think that Newfield's definition of the New Left as a prophetic minority defines a phenomenon that is both more subtle, and more massive, than this traditional pattern of outsiders' proposals permeating the status quo.

To begin with, Newfield understands that the youthful politics which he describes do not exist in isolation, that they are part of a much larger development in American (and even world) society. The Beats of the 1950's who disaffiliated rather than protested were prophets, too. Fewer in numbers than the New Left, confined to a few cities like San Francisco and New York, their extreme and committed alienation anticipated a mood that has since been expressed by the young people of America, of Europe, and even of Russia. Many proper middle-class people, and most of the magazines, dismissed the Beats as unwashed, bearded exhibitionists. In fact, they were the vanguard of a social and cultural revolution that can be seen today in teen-age dress styles as well as in the music of folk-rock and the lyrics of Bob Dylan.

Indeed, there is a sense in which it is always the untypical few who have the verve and energy to first articulate what is typical about their times. In the 1930's, for instance, as Murray Kempton has pointed out, the student Communists and Socialists were a relatively tiny percentage of the college population. Yet today, no one remembers the fraternity boys of the Depression. Those who went into the shop to help organize the CIO, or fought in Spain, or picketed against the war are the ones who speak to history about what those times were like.

I think Newfield's book captures the subtle, nonquantifiable way in which the New Leftists, for all of their problems and inadequacies, have captured one of the important essences of the sixties. There are, to be sure, only a few thousand who actively identify with the black and white poor, who reject affluence and go to the slums rather than to the suburbs for which their training and intelligence qualify them. These have a sort of mystique, a sense of oneness with all of the outcasts of the society, including even the junkie and the streetwalker.

Yet there is already the beginning of some solid evidence to document Newfield's insight about the prophetic function of these young people. In the spring of 1966, for instance, the Harris poll asked a cross section of college seniors what they wanted to do in life. Only 12 percent wanted a career in business; 24 percent looked to teaching; and 55 percent aimed at being professionals. A few years earlier, the *Wall Street Journal* reported, in shocked tones, that the students at an elite Ivy League university were more interested in the Peace Corps than in the corporations. In short, that most cherished principle of American life—that the business of this society is business—is no longer recognized, not simply by the New Leftists, but by a majority of the best educated young people in the nation.

This point, in turn, leads to the massive political implications of seeing these young people as prophets. For I think Newfield is quite right in asserting that the New Leftists are going to affect history.

Perhaps the first major political figure who benefited from, and even incarnated, the youthful mood of turning from business to service was John F. Kennedy. And it is significant that many of the New Leftists were first provoked into thought and commitment by the late President. They were to become disillusioned with the liberalism of the New Frontier as they turned to a more radical critique of American institutions. Yet the symbolic and catalytic role of Kennedy remains a most important fact in their collective autobiography. And this is a portent of the enormous practical political power that the idealism of the young possesses these days.

There are massive social and economic trends that make the political potential of the idealistic children of the middle class qualitatively greater than ever before in American history. A new, more sophisticated technology is shifting workers from industry to service, from blue collar to white, from semi-skilled assembly lines to highly skilled drawing boards. The effect of these transformations has been made all the more profound by the appearance in the labor market of the hordes of young people who have graduated from the postwar "baby boom" and are now adults. The entire nation has become younger.

There are many unhappy, even disastrous, consequences of these changes. The poor in the slums and the backwoods have, in a very real sense, fallen even farther behind the educational and skill requirements of the affluent. The economic progress of Negroes vis-à-vis whites, which was marked during and immediately after World War II, stopped, and perhaps even reversed direction, in the mid-fifties. And in the future, it is possible that the new occupational structure of the society will provide the basis of a two-class society of educated technocrats and janitors. If this were to happen, then the emergence of an unprecedented number of college graduates in the population would have the most reactionary consequences.

But there is another possibility, the one represented in a symbolic way by the New Leftists. For the young radicals, it is worth emphasizing, tend to be the brightest, the most restless and dynamic members of their generation. They are not malcontented rejects who are taking out their failure on society. Most of them have, for a while at least, consciously turned their backs on a success which they could easily achieve. This suggests that there may be a basis for a new "conscience politics" in the United States. Put in simple terms, this would mean that the spirit which impelled tens of thousands of white Americans to participate in various (and sometimes dangerous) aspects of the Negro struggle has become a national force. And that is not so fantastic.

Here, then, are the elements that lend substance to Newfield's conviction that his youthful prophets may play a practical, history-making role in American life. The best of the young have turned their backs on the elitist and crassly materialist implications of the new affluence. This radical rejection of the prevailing values is shared, in much more moderate form, by a significant portion of a collegiate generation which will make up an unprecedentedly large educated stratum in the America of tomorrow. And the possibility thus exists that the spirit, if not the letter, of the New Left could well become a practical political force in the United States of the 1970's.

In saying all of this, I do not for a moment want to imply an uncritical attitude toward the New Left or to suggest that its visions are soon to become the American political reality. Indeed, it is one of the very real accomplishments of Newfield's book that, although he is a partisan member of the generation he describes, he manages to be candid and honest about its inadequacies. And it seems to me that those seriously concerned with social change should talk plainly about these inadequacies—for that is the only way to overcome them.

The great gift which the New Left received from the Negro movement and, in turn, transmitted to the collegiate young of the middle class, was a sense of social outrage. The scandal of the Mississippi backwoods or of Harlem is so obvious once anyone bothers to notice it that no theories are required in order to react. The New Left applied this civil rights emotion and attitude to the problem of poverty, and then to the war in Vietnam. The result was an existential, moralistic, and quite emotional critique of the entire society and, in particular, a sense that the self-proclaimed reformers and social changers were hypocrites for maneuvering within the framework of the possible when what the times called for was a nonviolent John Brown.

It was this sense of outrage, generated by the Negroes, which destroyed the stultifying political and spiritual atmosphere of the Eisenhower fifties. But there was a danger in this development. Raw courage and determination were absolutely essential to those young people who took the Freedom Ride or faced death and imprisonment in the Mississippi summer of 1964. However, when the issues shifted to the complicated interrelationships of jobs, education, housing, the need for national planning, the way in which a truly effective poverty program could be developed, etc., political thought and strategy were desperately needed and sadly lacking.

The New Leftists sought to find Archimedean leverage points for social change, but only in those areas not dominated by the established liberal organizations. Essentially, they were searching for a new "proletariat" in the Marxian sense of the word: a social class that would be driven by the very conditions of its existence into a total transformation of the society; a group whose plight was so extreme that its definition of reform would be revolution. At first, the New Leftists thought that the collegians and the youth were such a proletariat; and then they sought it among the black and white poor. Yet the very changes in society which had opened up the possibility of a conscience politics on the part of an educated middle class had destroyed the possibility of a solidified and radical proletariat. For in the complicated economy of late capitalism, no group, not the workers, nor the middle class, nor the poor, is presently or incipiently strong enough to change the structure of society on its own. Politics could well become more radical under such circumstances, but they could only do so by way of a coalition among groups.

I think it is part of the great value of Newfield's book that he understands this point, that he realizes that eventually the New Left is going to have to radicalize the mainstream of society and take over the often unprophetic burdens of adult leadership. However, I hardly want to burden Jack Newfield with all of the specifics of my analysis, since we have differences of judgment and opinion between us. I am, for instance, a "Social Democrat" as that political tendency is described in this book. I am a personal friend and political collaborator of people like Bayard Rustin and Irving Howe and do not share Newfield's criticisms of them. I still feel that the "a-Communism" of the New Left is too agnostic a position in a world in which the bureaucratic collectivist society of Communism is both a model for forced industrialization (China) and for the continuation of dictatorship even after capital has been accumulated (Russia). And I believe that it is sociological inaccuracy and political suicide to dismiss the trade unions, which must be a major component of any new majority.

But, if I may invest a personal relationship with a political significance, the heartening thing to me is that Newfield and I have maintained a friendship despite our differences. We were arrested together in a sit-in in 1961; we were on opposite sides of the generational barricades in a faction fight in Students for a Democratic Society in 1962; and now, in 1966, I have the privilege of writing my own opinionated introduction to his excellent book. I am one of the few political survivors of that shellshocked generation of the fifties, and I have been bewildered and angered as well as heartened by the New Leftists. Yet I am convinced, as Jack Newfield is, that their great contribution is yet to come, and I look forward to that day when radicalism in America will be united and effective, a mass movement in the very center of the society.

For now, there is this thoughtful, committed evocation of the prophetic minority of our times. If Jack Newfield is right, the people described in this book will eventually help make American history—and I think he is right.

MICHAEL HARRINGTON

Preface

This book is an attempt to chronicle, describe, and analyze the growing mood and style of discontent among an important minority of young people. I have tried to write a document at once fraternally supportive of this New Radicalism and candidly critical of its excesses and shortcomings.

First, a few of the suppositions upon which this book is founded. There is now a deep disjunction between generations of American radicals. The older ideological Left—socialist and Communist—virtually withered away during the drought of the 1950's. A New Left then began slowly to take root, nourished by the pacifist and socialist British New Left of the Aldermaston Marches and the *New Left Review;* by the Beats' private disaffection from and rage at the Rat Race; by the Cuban revolution; and by the writings of such men as C. Wright Mills, Albert Camus, and Paul Goodman. This New Left blossomed dramatically in the spring of 1960 with the lunch-counter sit-ins, peace marches, capital-punishment protests, and a riot against the chief symbol of

McCarthyism—the House Un-American Activities Committee.

Defining this New Radicalism at its current youthful stage is a little like defining the infant abolitionist movement in 1850. Nevertheless, it seems, at bottom, an ethical revolt against the visible devils of racism, poverty, and war, as well as the less tangible devils of centralized decision-making, manipulative, impersonal bureaucracies, and the hypocrisy that divides America's ideals from its actions from Watts to Saigon.

The New Radicalism appears to be an attempt to add a wholly new communitarian and existential dimension to American politics by a generation that grew up during the years of Warsaw, Auschwitz, Hiroshima, Nuremberg, Seoul, and Budapest. Such events convinced many of us that all the old, pat leftist formulas had failed, and a new ethical politics was desperately required.

The New Left expresses this new ethical-rooted politics in its affirmation of community, honesty, and freedom, and in its indifference to ideology, discipline, economics, and conventional political forms.

What is explicitly *new* about the New Left is its ecumenical mixture of political traditions that were once murderous rivals in Russia, Spain, France, and the United States. It contains within it, and often within individuals, elements of anarchism, socialism, pacifism, existentialism, humanism, transcendentalism, bohemianism, Populism, mysticism, and black nationalism.

I define the New Radicalism broadly to include organizations like Students for a Democratic Society (SDS) and the Student Nonviolent Coordinating Committee (SNCC); *ad hoc* decentralized movements like the Berkeley Free Speech Movement (FSM) and the movement against the war in Vietnam. It includes idealistic Peace Corps and VISTA (domestic Peace Corps) volunteers and nihilistic Berkeley bohemians; new institutions like the Institute for Policy Studies and the Mississippi Freedom Democratic Party; new publications like *Liberation* and the *Southern Courier;* individuals like Bob Parris, Tom Hayden, and Staughton Lynd; it even spills over into sociocultural movements represented by Bob Dylan, Phil Ochs, Dr. Timothy Leary, and Allen Ginsberg.

In addition to the organizational New Left of radical activists, there is also an invisible layer to what is called the movement. This consists of recent college graduates and young intellectuals now tucked away in government agencies, publishing houses, faculties, graduate schools, and editorial offices. Perhaps uncomfortable with the gritty militance of the full-time radicals, these career-oriented sympathizers nevertheless share the New Radicals' basic values and assumptions about a commercial, militaristic, bureaucratic, and exclusive society.

However, I carefully distinguish from the New Left a phenomenon I call the Hereditary Left, represented by the Progressive Labor Party, the W. E. B. Du Bois Clubs, and the recently dissolved May 2nd Movement. I contend that despite surface similarities with the New Left, the Hereditary Left is actually an ideological extension of the old 1930's Left, is ideologically Leninist in structure and outlook, and is oriented toward either China or the Soviet Union rather than toward forging a new vision of American society.

The New Left includes probably no more than 250,000 people, between the ages of fifteen and thirty. It is only a minute—but intellectually gifted—fraction of a generation that has 5.2 millions of its members in colleges, and several millions more just graduated or about to enter a university. But I think it will be the fragment to give my generation (I am twenty-eight) its historical character, just as a visionary fragment gave the Lost and Beat Generations their identities.

My criticisms of the New Left are serious ones, but they do not detract from the ultimate validity of the movement. My reservations are of three basic types. One is that the New Radicals, while justified in most of their assaults on the Great Society, have been weak on providing creative alternatives. Occasionally they have been negative to the edge of nihilism. Two, they are sometimes hopelessly romantic, especially about unromantic aberrations like violence and authoritarianism. Some of them don't quite understand what nondemocratic socialism has done to the lives of those who live under its yoke; they don't quite understand the equal duplicity of the phrases "free world" and "national liberation." My third qualification is that segments of the New Left are anti-intellectual, sometimes even anti-rational. In the course of writing this book I have tried to raise these objections where they have seemed relevant, but I have also tried to keep them in balance with the positive totality of the movement.

Whatever biases this volume is burdened with come from my three philosophical premises: a belief in the democracy of Jefferson, the nonviolence of Camus, and the radical empiricism of William James. I believe in liberal values and radical action.

Finally, a few grateful acknowledgments.

To my mother, whose Old Testament morality long ago prepared me to empathize with the humanist values of the New Radicals.

To James Wechsler and Murray Kempton for being inspirations during that dreamless decade of few inspirations.

To Mike Harrington for being an example during this decade of abundant examples to choose from.

To Elizabeth Sutherland for giving me access to the SNCC files, and Carey McWilliams for his thoughtful flow of useful clippings.

To those who read the galleys and made constructive criticisms: Phil Hutchings, Bob Ross, Dick Flacks and Allard Lowenstein.

To friends, Tom and Casey Hayden; Paul and Rachel Cowan; and Carol Rogoff, who generously contributed important insights gained from their own experience in the movement.

To Linda, for being.

To Dan, for everything.

Chapter 1
The Movement

We want to create a world in which love is more possible.
—CARL OGLESBY, *SDS President*

*There is a time when the operation of the machine becomes so
odious, makes you so sick at heart that you can't take part; you
can't even tacitly take part, and you've got to put your bodies
upon the levers, upon all the apparatus, and you've got to make it
stop. And you've got to indicate to the people who run it, to the
people who own it, that unless you're free, the machine will be
prevented from working at all.*
—MARIO SAVIO, *leader of the FSM*

I can't get no satisfaction.
—THE ROLLING STONES

■ A new generation of radicals has been spawned from the
chrome womb of affluent America. The last lingering doubts that
the Silent Generation had found its voice vanished forever on
April 17, 1965, when more than 20,000 of this new breed converged on the nation's capital to protest against the war in Vietnam. It was the largest anti-war demonstration in the history of
Washington, D.C.—and it had been organized and sponsored by a
student organization—SDS.

Assembled in the warm afternoon sunshine that Saturday were
the boys and girls who had "freedom rode" to Jackson, Mississippi; who had joined the Peace Corps and returned disillusioned;
tutored Negro teen-agers in the slums of the great cities; vigiled
against the Bomb; rioted against the House Un-American Activities Committee; risked their lives to register voters in the Black
Belt; and sat-in for free speech at the University of California at
Berkeley.

They were the new generation of American radicals, nourished not by the alien cobwebbed dogmas of Marx, Lenin, and Trotsky, but by the existential humanism of Albert Camus, the Anti-colonialism of Frantz Fanon; the communitarian anarchism of Paul Goodman; the poetic alienation of Bob Dylan; and the grass-roots radicalism of that "prophetic shock minority" called SNCC. They were there not to protest anything so simple as war or capitalism. They came to cry out against the hypocrisy called Brotherhood Week, assembly lines called colleges, manipulative hierarchies called corporations, conformity called status, lives of quiet desperation called success.

They heard Joan Baez sing Dylan's sardonic poem, "With God on Our Side," and cheered spontaneously when she sang, "Although they murdered six million, in the ovens they fried/Now they too have God on their side."

They sang "Do What the Spirit Say Do," the latest freedom hit to come out of the jails and churches of the South, an indication perhaps of their deepest concern—human freedom and expression. Thus, Freedom now, "Oh Freedom," freedom ride, free university, freedom school, Free Speech Movement, and the Freedom Democratic Party.

And the 20,000 listened to the visionary voices of the New Radicalism.

Staughton Lynd, a romantic, a Quaker, and a revolutionary, told them:

> We are here today in behalf of Jean-Paul Sartre . . . we are here to keep the faith with those of all countries and all ages who have sought to beat swords into ploughshares and to war no more.

They heard Bob Parris, SNCC's humble visionary, who told them:

> Listen and think. Don't clap, please. . . . Don't use Mississippi as a moral lightning rod. Use it as a looking glass. Look into it and see what it tells you about all of America.

And they listened to Paul Potter, the tense, brilliant, twenty-four-year-old former president of SDS, who said:

There is no simple plan, no scheme or gimmick that can be proposed here. There is no simple way to attack something that is deeply rooted in the society. If the people of this country are to end the war in Vietnam, and to change the institutions which create it, then the people of this country must create a massive social movement—and if that can be built around the issue of Vietnam, then that is what we must do.

By a social movement I mean more than petitions and letters of protest, or tacit support of dissident Congressmen; I mean people who are willing to change their lives, who are willing to challenge the system, to take the problem of change seriously. By a social movement I mean an effort that is powerful enough to make the country understand that our problems are not in Vietnam, or China or Brazil or outer space or at the bottom of the ocean, but here in the United States. What we must begin to do is build a democratic and humane society in which Vietnams are unthinkable. . . .

Then, after three hours of speeches and freedom singing, the 20,000 stood in the lengthening shadow of the Washington Monument, linked arms, and, swaying back and forth, sang the anthem of their movement. Reaching out to clasp strange hands were button-down intellectuals from Harvard and broken-down Village hippies; freshmen from small Jesuit schools and the overalled kamikazes of SNCC; curious faculty members and high-school girls; angry ghetto Negroes and middle-aged parents, wondering what motivates their rebellious children; all together, singing and feeling the words, "Deep in my heart/ I do believe/ We shall overcome someday."

The SDS march, which had drawn twice the participation everyone, including its sponsors, had expected, suddenly illuminated a phenomenon that had been growing underground, in campus dorms, in the Mississippi delta, in bohemian subcultures, for more than five years. It was the phenomenon of students rejecting the dominant values of their parents and their country; becoming alienated, becoming political, becoming active, becoming radical; protesting against racism, poverty, war, Orwell's 1984, Camus' executioner, Mills' Power Elite, Mailer's Cancerous Totalitarianism; protesting against irrational anti-Communism, nuclear weaponry, the lies of statesmen, the hypocrisy of laws against narcotics and abortion; protesting against loyalty oaths, speaker bans, HUAC, *in loco parentis*—and finally, at Berkeley, protesting against the computer, symbol of man's dehumanization by the machine; in sum, protesting against all those obscenities that form the cryptic composite called the System.

In the weeks immediately following the SDS march the mass media suddenly discovered that the Brainwashed Generation, as poet Karl Shapiro had tagged the campus catatonics of the 1950's, had become a protest generation, that a cultural and sociological revolution had taken place while they had been preoccupied with the Bogart cult, J. D. Salinger, and baseball bonus babies. Within an eight-week period, *Time, Newsweek, The Saturday Evening Post, The New York Times Magazine, Life,* and two television networks all popularized the New Left. They smeared it, they psychoanalyzed it, they exaggerated it, they cartooned it, they made it look like a mélange of beatniks, potheads, and agents of international Communism; *they did everything but explain the failures in the society that called it into being.*

The New Radicalism is pluralistic, amorphous, and multi-layered. Its three political strands—anarchism, pacifism, and socialism—mingle in different proportions in different places. It's different in every city, on every campus. In Berkeley there is a strong sex-drug-literary orientation. In New York there is a politically sophisticated component. In the South there is extra emphasis on the nonviolent religious element.

At its surface, *political* level, the New Radicalism is an anti-Establishment protest against all the obvious inequities of American life. It says that Negroes should vote, that America should follow a peaceful, noninterventionist foreign policy, that anti-Communism at home has become paranoid and destructive, that the poverty of forty million should be abolished. It is a series of individual criticisms many liberals can agree with.

At its second, more complex level, this new movement is a *moral* revulsion against a society that is becoming increasingly corrupt. The New Radicals were coming to maturity as McCarthy built a movement based on deceit and bullying, as Dulles lied about the CIA's role in the 1954 Guatemala *coup*, as Eisenhower lied to the world about the U-2 flight over the Soviet Union, as Adlai Stevenson lied to the UN about America's support of the Bay of Pigs invasion, as Charles Van Doren participated in fixed quiz shows on television, as congressmen and judges were convicted for bribery. They saw the organs of masscult lie about their movement, the clergy exile priests for practicing brotherhood, older men red-bait their organizations. Feeling this ethical vacuum in the country, the New Radicals have made morality and truth the touchstones of their movement. Like Gandhi, they try to "speak truth to power." Their politics are not particularly concerned with power or success, but rather with absolute moral alternatives like love, justice, equality, and freedom. Practical, programmatic goals are of little interest. They want to pose an alternate vision, not just demand "more" or "better" of what exists. They don't say welfare programs should be better subsidized; they say they should be administered in a wholly different, more dignifying way. They don't say Negroes need leaders with better judgment; they say Negroes should develop spokesmen from their own ranks.

At its third, subterranean level, the New Radicalism is an *existential* revolt against remote, impersonal machines that are not responsive to human needs. The New Radicals feel sharply the growing totalitarianization of life in this technological, urban decade. They feel powerless and unreal beneath the unfeeling instruments that control their lives. They comprehend the essentially undemocratic nature of the military-industrial complex; the Power Elite; the multiversity with its IBM course cards; urban renewal by technocrats; canned television laughter; wire taps; automation; computer marriages and artificial insemination; and, finally, the mysterious button somewhere that can trigger the nuclear holocaust.

The New Radicals are the first products of liberal affluence. They have grown up in sterile suburbs, urban complexes bereft of community, in impersonal universities. They are the children of economic surplus and spiritual starvation. They agree with C. Wright Mills when he writes, "Organized irresponsibility, in this impersonal sense, is a leading characteristic of modern industrial societies everywhere. On every hand the individual is confronted with seemingly remote organizations; he feels dwarfed and helpless before the managerial cadres and their manipulated and manipulating minions."

And they can only chant "amen" to Lewis Mumford, who observed in *The Transformations of Man*, modern man has already depersonalized "himself so effectively that he is no longer man enough to stand up to his machines."

From their fury at arbitrary power wielded by impersonal machines (governments, college administrations, welfare bureaucracies, draft boards, television networks) come some of the New Radicals' most innovative ideas. Participatory democracy—the notion that ordinary people should be able to affect all the decisions that control their lives. The idea that social reformation comes from organizing the dispossessed into their own insurgent movements rather than from forming top-down alliances between liberal bureaucratic organizations. The insistence on fraternity and community inside the movement. The passion against manipulation and centralized decision-making. The reluctance to make the New Left itself a machine tooled and fueled to win political power in the traditional battle pits. The concept of creating new democratic forms like the Mississippi Freedom Democratic Party, the Newark Community Union Project, and the *Southern Courier*, a newspaper designed to represent the Negroes of the Black Belt rather than the white power structure or the civil-rights organizations. It is its brilliant insight into the creeping authoritarianism of modern technology and bureaucracy that gives the New Radicalism its definitive qualities of decentralism, communitarianism, and existential humanism.

Historically, the New Radicals' forebearers are the Whitman-Emerson-Thoreau transcendentalists, and the Joe Hill-Bill Hayward Wobblies. Like the IWW mill strikers at Lawrence, Massachusetts, in 1912, the New Left wants "bread and roses too."

Chapter 2

The
Beat Generation
And The
Un-Generation

The employers will love this generation. They aren't going to press many grievances. They are going to be easy to handle. There aren't going to be any riots.

—CLARK KERR, 1959

■ A time-capsule representative of the generation reaching adulthood during the 1950's would have consisted of a subpoena, a blacklist, a television tube, a gray flannel suit, a copy of *Time* magazine with Herman Wouk on the cover, a Lawrence Welk album, an "I like Ike" button, and a blank sheet of paper.

It was a decade during which a senator from Mississippi was able to bully the greatest newspaper in the world; a President's favorite reading was pulp cowboy novels; a Gallup Poll showed that 58 percent of all college students listed *Mad* as their favorite magazine; and an ex-socialist wrote a book called *The End of Ideology.* It was a time when potential poets read Jack Kerouac and potential radicals ran for student council.

It was a decade during which McCarthyism was the most vital political movement in the land, and liberalism, after two decades of creative exertion, had reached a point of pessimistic exhaustion. Many of the older liberal architects of the New Deal and the CIO were comfortably ensconced in labor bureaucracies and academic hierarchies. In the argot of the fight game, the liberals weren't hungry anymore.

McCarthyism had put the liberals on the defensive, making them wonder who had lost China and who had promoted Peress. Moreover, the liberals' idea bank was empty. The New Deal had used up all their intellectual capital, and now only slogans were left to cope with the new post-World War II problems of the anti-colonial revolution, the Cold War, nuclear proliferation, and technology and automation.

At the same time radicalism was at its absolute nadir. The Socialist Party was a shell. The cumulative blows of the Korean War, the Rosenbergs' conviction, the Smith Act trials, the Hungarian revolt, and the revelations about Stalin at the 20th Soviet Party Congress wrecked the Communist Party and its apparatus. In 1957 the Labor Youth League, the CP's youth arm, voted to dissolve.

Radicals were driven out of public life and liberals bullied into silence and conformity. *Time* magazine hailed the reconciliation between capitalist America and its intellectuals. The country seemed to be dozing in an easy chair after a great meal, belching intermittently to prove it was not quite asleep.

In its issue of March 9, 1957, at the height of the Silence, *The Nation* devoted an entire issue to reports from sixteen college campuses documenting the extraordinary apathy that afflicted the young. Stanley Kunitz, the poet and English professor at Queens College, wrote:

> However, I must add that when a liberal or speculative voice is heard in the classroom, it is more likely than not to be the professor's, despite whatever caution the years might have taught him. As for the students, they matriculate cautious, wanting above all—so well conditioned are they by the prevailing social climate—to buy security for themselves in the full knowledge that the price is conformity. "Why should we go out on a limb about anything?" one of them remarked

in class. "We know what happened to those who did." Another expressed a measure of gratitude towards Senator McCarthy for having taught his generation a valuable lesson: "to keep its mouth shut."

Poet Karl Shapiro, writing from the University of Nebraska, the crucible of the Norris-LaFollette Progressivism, commented:

> Passivity is the last word we expect to use in connection with a generation of students, but that's the only word that applies to the American university student of the last few years.

Perhaps the sharpest evocation of the dead feeling of the 1950's came in an article that appeared in an obscure periodical called *Assay*, published by the University of Washington. It was written by a co-ed named Dorothy Kosobud Doe, and it said in part:

> What we all lack who are under 30, is some guiding passion, some moral vision if you will. We are unable to wind the loose threads of our experience into some larger pattern, and we know it. We write to please this authority or that professor while the universe skids about under our feet. We profess to disbelieve everything partially because, at heart, we do not yet believe in ourselves. What we are facing is a process of re-education, of self-discovery—a painful process, but without it no human being has understood the reason for his short walk across eternity . . . if our revolt seems mild, it is because we have not found anything to promote; deep in the dreams of ourselves in our relation to others, we realize with Yeats that there's more enterprise in walking naked.

Why the 1950's did not provide rebellious, sensitive souls like Dorothy with "some guiding passion" or "anything to promote" is a mystery. Why the New Left didn't emerge then, when there was a virulent right-wing that threatened to become a majority, when there was a series of economic recessions, when there were atrocities like the lynchings of Emmett Till and Mack Charles Parker, and when there was an unthawed Cold War, is an enigma of history. That the New Radicalism flowered *after* the death rattle of McCarthyism and during a period of remarkable prosperity contradicts most theories about the nature of social discontent and rebellion.

My own suspicion is that rebellion explodes not when repression is at its worst, but when it begins to ebb, when the possibility of something better is dimly glimpsed. Both the American and the Hungarian revolutions took place when conditions were beginning to improve. The same is true of the birth of the New Left here. It happened after Khrushchev's visit to America and after the liberal victories in the 1958 congressional elections.

The election of John Kennedy in 1960 probably hastened the flowering of the New Radicalism. In that election the nation chose vitality over torpor, adventure over caution, hope over passivity; and this decision liberated energies bottled up for a decade. If Nixon had won in 1960, I think the earliest protests would have been crushed in a McCarthyite paroxysm and the New Left aborted. Kennedy provided a friendly umbrella for the New Left to grow under, and held up a vision of social idealism, represented by the Peace Corps, which led students to take the logical next step—into SNCC and SDS.

My own undergraduate experience at Hunter College in the Bronx was foreshadowed by a sign I saw during my freshman semester (1956) on the bulletin board in the office of the student newspaper, the *Hunter Arrow*. The sign read bluntly, "Conform or Die."

Hunter was lucky enough during the McCarthy plague to have a liberal Catholic president, Dr. George N. Shuster. But the college had neither the radical tradition of CCNY, Antioch, or Berkeley, nor the rich intellectual tradition of Harvard, Chicago, or Michigan. The students, mostly lower middle class and Jewish, reflected their families and their times. They were fearful and conformist. During my later terms on the *Arrow* we officially banned the use of the word "apathy" because it had been so over-worked in shrill editorials of exhortation.

Few of the three thousand undergraduates joined any of the myriad campus clubs and organizations, a lesson absorbed from the "don't sign and don't join" McCarthy experience. We all re-membered the State Department employee McCarthy pilloried because of editorials he had written for the *Columbia Spectator* and petitions he had signed twenty-five years before. When speakers like Norman Thomas came to the campus they addressed seventy-five students and hundreds of vacant auditorium seats. At Hunter, politics meant running for student council on an innocu-ous platform, and dissent meant a vague, emotional yearning for Adlai Stevenson. The life pattern today's campus rebels recoil from in disgust, my classmates deified: marry well and early, don't be a troublemaker, start a career in daddy's business or in a large corporation, and save up for a split-level home in the lily-white suburbs.

The vast majority of my classmates just sat through four years. They didn't challenge any authority, take any risks, or ask any questions. They just memorized "the given," not even complain-ing when instructors turned them into mindless tape recorders, demanding they recite rather than reason. They seemed genu-inely content with the world, and interested only in being re-warded with a painless niche in it. They signed loyalty oaths without complaint in order to receive college loans. When the administration suggested stringent dress regulations on the cam-pus, the student council meekly voted to ratify this infringement on their liberties. When a maverick political science instructor was denied tenure and left, no one protested.* Most of my class-

* By 1961, however, attitudes had changed. Eighty-five percent of the Hunter student body supported a strike against the City University speaker ban, which denied Communists, black nationalists, and others the right to speak on campuses.

mates became teachers, accountants, press agents, housewives, and salesmen.

No public question seemed to touch Hunter's class of '60; not McCarthyism, not Dulles' brinksmanship, not pollution of the atmosphere by nuclear testing, not even the nascent integration movement. They were worse than a Silent Generation or an Uncommitted Generation—they were an Un-generation.

They were an Un-generation in the sense that nothing positive distinguished them or set them apart. They were bereft of passions, of dreams, of gods. Even their small, conventional expectations were squeezed out of the same label-less tube. If any single characteristic bound them together it was withdrawal. Not the experimental, alienated withdrawal of the Beats, but a timid, unfeeling withdrawal. They withdrew from conflict and emotion into a false, protective, "cool" detachment. They took up the pose of the jazz buff who dug the "cool jazz" of Brubeck and Getz. They carried around paperbacks by clinical and unfeeling novelists like William Golding and the latest example of *The New Yorker* school of bloodless, overdetailed fiction. And their *Zeitgeist*—J. D. Salinger—stood for a total withdrawal from reality into the womb of childhood, innocence, and mystical Zen. Most of my contemporaries even managed to sustain their withdrawal beyond graduation, drifting off to Europe or going on to take meaningless graduate courses.

There were, I suspect, deeper reasons for the Un-generation's withdrawal than the intimidation by McCarthyism and the collapse of an energizing liberalism. One such reason seems to have been the instructive image of a passive President who withdrew from the world's problems. Just as John Kennedy's celebrated vigor ignited the country's spirit in 1960, I think Eisenhower's inability to deal with segregation, Laos, Eastern Europe, the economy, McCarthy, and the rest created a sense of futility in the country at large.

A second underlying cause of the Silence was the often-forgotten fact that American youth has never been particularly political in the way that Latin American, Asian, and European youth have. There was no dramatic upsurge of youthful radicalism accompanying the Progressive movement, the Populists, the abolitionists, or the American Revolution itself. American youth has no tradition of vanguard radicalism. One of the more subtle inspirations to the New Left was, I think, the catalytic role students played in 1960 in overthrowing the reactionary regimes of Menderes in Turkey and Syngman Rhee in Korea.

The last of the deeper reasons for the Silence was probably the traditional banality of the American campus and student-government politics. Until quite recently campus politics were insulated from "outside issues" like war, civil rights, and poverty; they have been a substitute for, rather than a supplement to, the substantive national politics of the country. Indicatively, the FSM had at its core the notion of replacing real issues in the real world for the vacuity of campus politics. Also, I suspect that the traditional style of campus sandbox politics tended to reinforce the feeling of helplessness and futility in coping with the adult world of complex, worldly issues. Campus politics were constructed to prepare Joe College to become a docile Organization Man.

> The psychopath is a rebel without a cause, an agitator without a slogan, a revolutionary without a program: in other words his rebelliousness is aimed to achieve goals satisfactory to himself alone; he is incapable of exertions for the sake of others.
>
> —Dr. Robert Lindner

It was a bone-chilling November night during my junior year at Hunter. The college auditorium was packed tight for a debate on "Is There a Beat Generation?" The combatants were British novelist Kingsley Amis; James Wechsler, the liberal hero of my youth; anthropologist Ashley Montague; and the alleged "King of the Beats," novelist Jack Kerouac. From the start it was clear that much of the leotard and beard-freckled mob (mostly non-Hunter types) had come to cheer the King of the Beats, look over Amis as a possible Angry Young Man, and scorn the committed liberalism of Wechsler as a delusion for squares and do-gooders.

But Kerouac disappointed his disciples. Gulping brandy compulsively, dragging poet Allen Ginsberg out of the wings like a donkey, reciting doggerel about Harpo Marx and clowning with Wechsler's hat, Kerouac seemed more in harmony with the clown spirit of his "beloved Harpo" than with the merchandised image of the creative, adventuristic, iconoclastic Beats.

When asked from the audience to "define the Beat Generation," Kerouac belched drunkenly, "Being Beat goes back to my ancestors, to the rebellious, the weird, the mad. To Laurel and Hardy, to Popeye; to Lamont Cranston, the Shadow, with his insane heh-heh-heh laugh. . . ."

Wechsler, the optimistic liberal, could only respond to Kerouac's premature Camp by sputtering, "I think what you are doing is to try to destroy anybody's instinct to care about this world. . . . There is no valor in the Beats' flight and irresponsibility."

Wechsler, of course, was right, and the irrational, impotent dissent of Kerouac that night at Hunter was a fairly accurate example of the Beat Generation. The Beats were not political or effective, and except for Ginsberg and William Burroughs, not very creative. They were the children of futility. They withdrew from society into an anti-social subculture, instead of challenging and trying to change the society. But with the traditional voices of dissent mute, the Beat Generation became the only option for those in opposition. The Beats may have been rebels without a cause, but theirs was the only rebellion in town.

The Beat Generation was partly a small literary faction that centered around an in-group of friends. Kerouac, who according to critic Seymour Krim "single-handedly created the Beat Generation," was the leader. The more gifted followers included Allen Ginsberg, the Jewish-radical-mystical-homosexual from Paterson,

New Jersey; Gregory Corso, whom critic Robert Mazzocco once labeled, "The Shelley of the Mafia;" and William Burroughs, junkie, petty criminal, and dark genius out of the millionaire Burroughs adding-machine family and Harvard, '36.

The Beat movement was also a sociological phenomenon; an underground subsociety that developed about 1953, was mythicized by the Beat novelists and poets, and quickly spawned colonies in North Beach, San Francisco; Venice West, Los Angeles; Greenwich Village, New York; and outposts in Mexico City, Paris, and Tangiers. Its full-timers ranged from dreamy teen-agers on the bum to maladjusted Korean war veterans to jazzmen, criminals, and peyote-inspired poets. Each weekend its ranks would be swollen with Bronx boys picking up Brooklyn girls on MacDougal Street in the Village. At its periphery Beat just meant sloppy dress, inter-racial dating and poetry read to jazz backgrounds. At its vortex it meant criminality, mainline drug addiction, and mental instability. Lawrence Lipton, the Beats' Boswell, wrote: "One of the things which distinguish the holy barbarians [the Beats] from the respectable poets is their insistence on the non-rational as a way of knowing and a therapy to overcome squareness."

Allen Ginsberg, who saw "the best minds of my generation destroyed by madness," once spent eight months in a mental institution. Later he dedicated his brilliant work, *Howl*, to the institutionalized Carl Solomon. Seymour Krim wrote a chilling essay, "The Insanity Bit," after he "flipped out." And Kerouac was discharged from the Navy as a "schizoid personality."

A study of the San Francisco Beat enclave by psychiatrist Dr. Francis Rigney in the late 1950's showed 60 percent "were so psychotic or crippled by tensions, anxiety and neurosis as to be nonfunctional in the competitive world." In contrast, the several studies released so far made of the student radicals at Berkeley show them to be stable, serious, and of above-average intelligence. The point is that the Beats had to "cop out" of the Rat Race because they couldn't perform; the New Left chooses to reject a society it could easily be successful in.

The Beat Generation was anything but a revolutionary thrust to create a new society. It was as hostile to politics as it was to police and employment agencies. I recall asking one of Hunter's few authentic Beats to join the 1959 Youth March for Integrated Schools, and his laconic response, "You're too enthusiastic, man. Cool it."

The closest the Beats came to politics was to write bad poetry against the Bomb. But even this was more in the nature of self-justification for their own immediate savoring of all experience than a moral or political outcry against the shadow of genocide. Paul Goodman, generally sympathetic to the Beat impulse, pointed out in *Growing Up Absurd* that the Beats were no more against nuclear warfare than "mothers with families or squares who have common sense." And critic George Dennison, in putting down a Beat poem about the Bomb, observed, "The poet seems miffed that people pay attention to the atom bomb instead of to him."

Perhaps because the Beats—as writers and participants—didn't threaten anybody politically, the Beat Generation ended up as a Madison Avenue and Hollywood gimmick. The beatnik joined the plump suburban matron and the jowly business tycoon as a stock cartoon figure; slouched, bearded, and mumbling, "Like, man. . . ." A New York entrepreneur went into business renting out "real live beatniks" at twenty-five dollars per evening, plus carfare. *Playboy Magazine* had a "Beat Playmate of the Month." Hollywood ground out a Grade Z epic called *The Beat Generation* and an artless adaptation of Kerouac's novel, *The Subterraneans*. And the July, 1959, issue of *The Saturday Evening Post* featured a short story by Harriet Frank called, "Beauty and the Beatnik," whose hero declaims, "Let's face it. I'm a beatnik, through and through. James Jones. Jack Kerouac. They're Dun and Bradstreet compared to me. I'm a real bum."

Still, despite their absurdity and ultimate commercialization, many of the values of the Beats have been absorbed into the broader stream of the New Left. The Beats seem to be a greater influence on the New Radicals than are the 1930's Left.

On many campuses today hipster and bohemian types serve as a sort of *lumpen* proletariat, an easily available army of bodies, ready to participate in any demonstration. But they are generally not the creative and stable leaders of movements; rather the un-disciplined followers who get interviewed by cynical television reporters. SNCC's Texas-born Casey Hayden has a point when she says, "The beatniks were—and are—just the Movement without altruism and energy. They are alienated by exactly the same things we are, but they just can't act on their discontent in an effective political way."

Nevertheless, the Beats' mysticism, anarchy, anti-intellectual-ism, sexual and drug experimentation, hostility to middle-class values, and idealization of the Negro and of voluntary poverty all have clear parallels in the New Left. Moreover, there is a broad area of overlap between the Beats' creative expressions and the cultural tastes of the New Left. Individuals like Bob Dylan, Paul Krassner, and Allen Ginsberg serve as bridges between the two traditions. And within the New Left there is considerable liking for writers like Norman Mailer and Jean Genet; musical rebels like the Beatles and the half-rock'n'roll, half-pornographic Fugs; and for underground film-makers like Kenneth Anger. Both movements represent a rebellion against Puritanism, hypocrisy, repression, and commercialism. Only the Beats were apolitical, self-indulgent, and a bit mad, while the New Left has a moral vision of a new society and is trying to create it with social activ-ism.

More than anything else, the Beat Generation was a portent, the first wind of a new storm, a coded signal that America's youth was starting to gag on conformity, materialism, and silence. By the end of the 1950's there were not only the subcultures of Beats, but the irreverent satire of Lenny Bruce and Mort Sahl, the stirrings of SANE, Martin Luther King's local protests against segregation, and the slow growth of dissident publications like *I. F. Stone's Weekly*, *The Village Voice*, and *The Realist*.

This subtle new mood, which was to spawn the sit-in movement in 1960, was clearly perceived by Arthur Schlesinger, Jr., in a prophetic essay penned late in 1959 and called, "The New Mood in Politics." Perhaps thinking already of John Kennedy's bid for the Presidency, he wrote:

> At periodic moments in our history, our country has paused on the threshold of a new epoch in our national life, unable for a moment to open the door, but aware that it must advance if it is to preserve its national vitality and identity. One feels that we are approaching such a moment now. . . .
>
> The beginning of a new political epoch is like the breaking of a dam. Problems which have collected in the years of indifference, values which have suffered neglect, energies which have been denied employment— all suddenly tumble as in a hopeless, swirling flood onto an arid plain. . . .

The Beat Generation was the first trickle of the angry flood that is now promising to wash away so many of America's false totems, and cleanse so many of its rotted institutions.

Chapter 3
The Beginning

There is nothing so powerful in all the world as an idea whose time has come.

—Victor Hugo

What defines the radical possibilities, today as yesterday, is not a style of thought, or an intellectual trend. It is people in movement.

—Michael Harrington

■ Day-to-day life for the Southern Negro in the winter of 1960 was little different than it had been the year before, or five years before.

The pace of public-school desegregation was still proceeding at 1 percent per year, which meant that full compliance with Brown v. Board of Education would be achieved, "with all deliberate speed," by 2054. There were still more than forty counties in the South where not a single Negro was registered to vote, and more than twenty counties where white registration exceeded 100 percent. Negroes were still denied the right to use the same lunch counters, motels, theaters, and public toilets as whites. The White Citizens' Councils, founded in Mississippi in 1954, were growing rapidly. The lynchings of Emmett Till and Mack Charles Parker were still unsolved. Negro cotton-choppers were still paid three dollars a day in the Mississippi delta. Negro youth unemployment in cities like Birmingham and Atlanta was as high as 30 percent.

The 381-day Montgomery bus boycott; the federally enforced

integration of Little Rock's Central High; the eviction of Negro tenant farmers in Fayette County, Tennessee, for trying to vote were simply a prologue to the epic drama about to unfold. What happened in Greensboro, North Carolina, on February 1st, went unreported in *The New York Times* the next day, but it had the effect of the Boston Tea Party. It was the single spark that was to ignite the conscience of white America and the hope of black America. The four freshmen from a Jim Crow college who sat-in that day in Greensboro's downtown F. W. Woolworth could hardly sense the historic significance of their deed. No one, not John Kennedy, then starting his bid for the Presidency, not Martin Luther King, then a Moses without a movement, not George Wallace, then running for governor of Alabama, could know that a simple plea for a cup of coffee would set into motion a chain of events whose final meaning, six years later, is still shrouded beyond the rim of history.

On Sunday night, January 31st, four freshmen at all-Negro North Carolina Agricultural and Technical College, in Greensboro, relaxed in a dorm in Scott Hall, discussing the problem. Ezell Blair, Jr., chairman of the Student Committee for Justice, was one of them. The other three were David Richmond, seventeen, of Greensboro; Franklin McCain, eighteen, of Washington, D.C.; and Joseph McNeill, seventeen, of Wilmington, North Carolina.

The quartet, according to Blair, "spent a lot of time discussing the segregated situations we were exposed to. . . . It just didn't seem right that we would have to walk two miles to town, buy notebook paper and toothpaste in a national chain store, and then not be able to get a bite to eat and a cup of coffee at the counter."

On Sunday night the same dehumanizing experiences were being recited again when Joe McNeill exclaimed, "Well, we've talked about it long enough. Let's do something."

The four decided to "do something" the next day. They told no one of their decision.

At about 4:45 P.M. on February 1st, the four freshmen entered the F. W. Woolworth Company store on North Elm Street in the heart of the city. Each of them purchased a tube of toothpaste and then sat down at the lunch counter.

A Negro woman working in the kitchen rushed over to them and said, "You know you're not supposed to be in here." Later the woman called the four "ignorant" and a "disgrace to their race."

The students requested four cups of coffee from the white waitress.

"I'm sorry but we don't serve colored here," she informed them politely.

Franklin McCain responded, "I beg your pardon, but you just served me at a counter two feet away. Why is it that you serve me at that counter, and deny me at another? Why not stop serving me at all the counters?"

A few minutes later the manager of the store told the youths, "I'm sorry but we can't serve you because it is not the local custom."

The four young Negroes remained at the counter, coffeeless, until 5:30 P.M., when the store closed.

The next day, Tuesday, February 2nd, sixteen other North Carolina A and T undergraduates joined the four pioneers at the lunch counter. They were all denied service, and returned on Wednesday, fifty strong, including Negro high-school students from Dudley High and a few white co-eds from Women's College in Greensboro.

By Friday, February 5th, the integrated group had grown so large that some of them sat-in at an S. H. Kress store, one block away. They, too, were refused service. On Friday a large group of white high-school toughs in black leather jackets, carrying Confederate flags, began to heckle the students.

The confrontation was repeated on Saturday afternoon, when several hundred students, many carrying Bibles and all well dressed, sat-in and were surrounded by taunting white teen-agers.

At about 3 P.M. the management of Woolworth received a bomb threat, and the tense police used that as the pretext for emptying the store of both demonstrators and hecklers.

The students then marched to the Kress store. The manager met them in the doorway and shouted, "This store is closed, as of now."

The students cheered, feeling they had won a victory. "It's all over," they shouted. But it had really just begun. An idea's time had come.

The next week there were spontaneous sit-in demonstrations in many parts of North Carolina—Durham, Raleigh, Charlotte, Winston-Salem, High Point, Salisbury, and Concord. By Wednesday, February 10th, the movement had spilled over the border into Rock Hill and Orangeburg, in South Carolina. In Rock Hill a Negro boy was knocked off a stool by a white teenager, and ammonia was hurled through the door of a drugstore, bringing tears to the eyes of the students.

The sit-ins next swept into Hampton, Richmond, and Portsmouth, in Virginia. The first arrests came on February 12th in Raleigh, North Carolina, where forty-three students, including several whites, were jailed on charges of trespassing.

Twelve days after Greensboro, forty students, including John Lewis, future chairman of SNCC, sat-in at Woolworth's in Nashville, during a snowstorm. On February 27th, seventy-six people sat-in in Nashville. Lighted cigarettes were jabbed at the necks of several girls by segregationist hecklers. A white student from Vanderbilt University was dragged off his stool and pummeled. Paul LePrad, a Negro student at Fisk University, was pulled from his stool by a white adult and punched in the mouth. He got up and climbed back on his stool. By the end of the day all seventy-six had been jailed.

In Orangeburg, South Carolina, students at Claffin College and nearby South Carolina State held a series of workshops and seminars in nonviolence. On March 14th in Orangeburg, lunch counters were reopened after a month's closing, and seven hundred

students marched nonviolently downtown. Police met them with
tear-gas bombs and fire hoses. Dozens were knocked off their
feet and slammed against walls by high-pressure hoses that tore
the bark off tree stumps. More than 500 were arrested, and 350 of
them were locked into an eight-feet-high chicken coop because
the jails were full. The next day *The New York Times* carried a
front-page picture of the 350 huddling in the chicken-coop stockade, in subfreezing temperatures—singing "God Bless America."

By the first anniversary of the Greensboro sit-in, the NAACP
reported it had paid for the legal defense of seventeen hundred
demonstrators during the intervening year. According to Howard Zinn, in *The New Abolitionists*, more than 50,000 people participated in some kind of civil rights protest in the twelve months
after Greensboro, and "over 3600 demonstrators spent time in
jail."

It is impossible to overestimate the impact of those first, hardly
noticed sit-ins. Harold Flemming, who was director of the Southern Regional Council in 1960, said recently, "Just as the Supreme
Court decision was the legal turning point, the sit-ins were the
psychological turning point in race relations in the South."

Ralph McGill, the beacon of Atlanta liberalism, did not at first
support the sit-in movement. But a few years later, in his book,
The South and the Southerner, he wrote:

> The sit-ins were, without question, productive of the most
> change. . . . No argument in a court of law could have
> dramatized the immorality and irrationality of such a custom
> as did the sit-in. . . . The sit-ins reached far out into the
> back country. They inspired adult men and women, fathers,
> mothers, grandmothers, aunts and uncles, to support the
> young students in the cities. Not even the Supreme Court
> decision on schools in 1954 had done this. . . .

The sit-in technique was not invented in Greensboro. The
Gandhi-influenced Congress of Racial Equality (CORE) had

used it successfully in Chicago, in 1942, and again in St. Louis, in 1949.

Greensboro was not a particularly backward city in terms of race relations. Its public schools desegregated voluntarily in 1955, and both daily newspapers were to come out against lunch-counter segregation after the sit-ins began.

It all seemed to be the caprice of history that the spontaneous sit-in on February 1st in Greensboro should give off sparks that showered the South, igniting local protests in sixty-five communities in twelve states within six weeks. Perhaps the Greensboro sit-in was merely the catalyst that needed to be added to the existing chemicals of the 1954 school desegregation decision, the Montgomery bus boycott, and the emerging nations of Africa, in order to liberate the dammed-up rivers of idealism, energy, and courage that cascaded through the South those first weeks of 1960.

A few years ago Ezell Blair, Jr., one of the first Greensboro sit-inners, recalled, "It seems as if it's all a dream since the first sit-in, although deep back in my mind I thought it would grow."

The early sit-in activist was surprisingly middle class and patriotic. He was always well groomed and wore a suit and tie when demonstrating. Often he read the Bible or a copy of the Constitution while sitting at the lunch counter. If he broke his disciplined decorum to sing at the moment of arrest, it was often a patriotic anthem.

An early sit-in leader from Alabama State College told me in 1960, "The point of our protest, as I see it, is to prove to the white people we aren't children and deserve our full and equal rights. The sit-in technique shows these whites we can do without immediate gratification, unlike children, and that we can wait like adults for our rights."

That first-generation activist was only distantly related to the SNCC worker I saw on the Selma-to-Montgomery march, in sunglasses, goatee, mud-caked boots, and field overalls, singing, "Do

What the Spirit Say Do," while a melody by the Supremes pranced out of a transistor radio jammed against his ear.

Because the students in Greensboro, Orangeburg, and Nashville were so square and respectable, what they did was perhaps even more heroic than the deeds of the current radicals in the movement. *More* heroic because those kids only wanted their share of the middle-class American Dream—success, prestige, and money —and they were willing to risk what they wanted most in wrenching loose from everything they had been taught by conservative parents, paternalistic college presidents, and timorous Negro leaders. It would seem to be much easier for the current movement swingers, who despise the middle-class tokens of success, to go to jail and jeopardize careers than it was for those cautious children of the black bourgeoisie who sang "God Bless America" in the Orangeburg stockade.

Even the segregationists were forced to marvel at the Sunday School decorum of the sit-in activists. The states' rights champion, the *Richmond News Leader*, commented editorially on February 22, 1960:

> Many a Virginian must have felt a tinge of wry regret at the state of things as they are, in reading of Saturday's "sitdowns" by Negro students in Richmond stores. Here were the colored students, in coats, white shirts, ties, and one of them was reading Goethe and one was taking notes from a biology text. And here, on the sidewalk outside, was a gang of white boys come to heckle, a ragtail rabble, slack-jawed, black-jacketed, grinning fit to kill, and some of them, God save the mark, were waving the proud and honored flag of the Southern States in the last war fought by gentlemen.

From the third day of the sit-ins in Greensboro, the movement was inter-racial. The shock waves radiating from North Carolina quickly jolted Northern campuses out of a decade's silence and sloth. The television newsreels of fellow students being punched by hecklers and hosed by police pierced the split-level dream of thousands of white Northern students. On Lincoln's Birthday, about fifty Hunter College students joined a sympathy picket line of one thousand outside an F. W. Woolworth branch on 125th Street in Harlem. Students at Rutgers, Berkeley, Minnesota, Yale, and Antioch rushed to centers of sit-in activity to get arrested. University of Connecticut students collected two hundred dollars at a campus rally and sent it to Raleigh after the first arrests. David Koulack of Brandeis University and Michael Walzer of Harvard (now a writer and academic) made trips to the South, returned, and organized support movements on their home campuses. In an estimated 130 cities and hamlets of the North, whites, mostly students, demonstrated in solidarity with their brothers in the South. The Uncommitted Generation was beginning to find a commitment; the Silent Generation was beginning to find its voice on a picket line; and the generation that wouldn't sign a petition was beginning to realize a jail record could be a badge of honor. In those first few weeks, the sit-ins clearly liberated more white middle-class students in the North than it did Southern Negroes.

But even in the South, white students were rallying to the fledgling movement. Greensboro College co-eds had joined the Woolworth sit-in on its third day. Candie Anderson, a co-ed at Fisk University, had been among the leaders of the Nashville movement. In Jacksonville, Florida, a white student jailed during a sit-in had his jaw broken in jail by another prisoner. And in the March 16th issue of the University of North Carolina student newspaper, the *Daily Tarheel,* associate editor Frank Crowther wrote in an editorial:

"I believe the Negro is right and I will support him in his heartfelt protestations, which are based on law, order and peaceful resistance. I believe he has an unequivocally valid position—the law grants him equality while the Southern white denies it. Thus the Negro is born under one law and forced to live under another. He is openly attempting to alleviate his situation by peaceful and non-violent means. He is publicly appealing for something which has been cruelly expropriated from him. I believe in his quest."

Within a year the SNCC staff was to contain native-born, white Southerners like Bob Zellner, Jane Stembridge, Casey Hayden, and Sam Shirah. And later, in 1964, white Southerners like Ed Hamlet, Sue Thrasher, Howard Romaine and Gene Guerrero were to found the Southern Student Organizing Committee (SSOC). Its purpose: to educate, agitate, and demonstrate against segregation and poverty among Negroes and whites.

The sit-ins were a student movement, conceived, planned, and carried out by students who wanted their rights. They were a rejection of the legalism of the NAACP and the gradualism of the Uncle Toms. They were an affirmation of the passive-resistance movement built by Martin Luther King in Montgomery, Alabama.

From the beginning the students received tutoring in nonviolence and tactical coaching from both CORE and Martin Luther King's Southern Christian Leadership Conference (SCLC). Before the first week of sit-ins ended in Greensboro, CORE's Len Holt arrived in town to conduct workshops in nonviolence, where potential demonstrators were tested in role-playing to see if they could remain nonviolent in face of taunts, shoves, and kicks. Also, Martin Luther King himself came to Greensboro to lend inspiration and moral prestige to the students' movement.

Even though the movement was quite respectable, middle class, and, by today's standards, nonradical, it nevertheless generated deep cleavages within the Negro community. In many cities, Nashville and Savannah specifically, the NAACP sought to contain the sit-ins and tried to negotiate settlements with white merchants, which the students later rejected. Many sit-in leaders were told by their parents they were disgracing their race. John Lewis, who was a seminary student in Nashville when the sit-ins erupted, received a letter from his mother demanding that he get out of the movement. The twenty-one-year-old Lewis wrote back:

"I have acted according to my convictions and according to my Christian conscience. . . . My soul will not be satisfied until freedom, justice and fair play become a reality for all people."

The strongest opposition to the sit-ins came from the presidents of state-supported Negro colleges, like Southern University in Baton Rouge. The president there was Dr. Felton Clark, who had held the post since 1938, when he took it over from his father. Many of the students believed he was the prototype for Dr. Bledsoe, the Uncle Tom college president in Ralph Ellison's *Invisible Man*.

In early March the all-white State Board of Education, which administered Southern University, issued a warning that any student participating in a sit-in would be subject to "stern disciplinary action." The movement had not yet spread to Baton Rouge, but as Ronnie Moore, until recently a CORE field secretary, put it, "When the Board spoke, it became a challenge to us and we couldn't ignore it."

On March 28th, seven Southern University students sat-in at a Kress lunch counter and were arrested within twenty minutes. The next day nine students sat-in at a drugstore and at the Greyhound bus terminal. On March 30th, President Clark expelled the sixteen sit-inners, plus another student, Major Johns, who had addressed a mass rally of students in support of the movement.

More than 3,000 Southern University students boycotted classes for a week to protest the expulsions, and almost 1,000 quit the university by Easter vacation in protest.

Similarly, forty students who participated in the movement were expelled from all-Negro Albany State College in Albany, Georgia. Students were also expelled from Florida Agricultural and Mining College and Alabama State College in Montgomery. Noted Negro History Professor L. D. Reddick was forced to leave Alabama State because of his active support of the students.*

Such actions must have been in the mind of Martin Luther King when he told a mass rally in a Raleigh church in April, "The sit-in movement is a revolt against those Negroes in the middle class who have indulged themselves in big cars, and ranch-style homes, rather than joining in the movement for freedom."

Many of the characteristics that have come to define the New Left were visible, in embryo form, in the sit-in movement, despite its solemnity, narrow vision, and middle-class orientation.

The sit-ins, firstly, were a moral rather than economic or political protest, a kind of mass vomit against the hypocrisy of segregation. Today, most of the movement's demonstrations retain this quality of retching upon a system that literally makes many young people sick to their stomachs. The idea of economic punishment of dime-store chains that discriminate came from the North, and the sit-in movement never became overtly political.

The sit-ins, too, were a spontaneous, unplanned activist contagion. They gave people something to do immediately to show their feelings about segregation. They required no ideology, no politics, and no scholarship—just one's body and a certain set of ethical values. Today, these remain the lowest common denominators among the young activists.

The sit-ins were an assertion of individual freedom, the right to eat a hamburger where one chooses. That they began at a lunch counter rather than at a welfare office, an unemployment office, a police station, or a mayor's office was appropriate, although probably accidental. Today the New Left remains basically preoccupied with questions of individual freedom: freedom of the very poor from arbitrary power, freedom to vote, freedom to organize, and the philosophical question itself of what freedom means. Deep into the night SNCC and SDS workers often debate the

* For an analysis of southern Negro colleges see "The Unfamiliar Campus," by Staughton Lynd and Roberta Yancy, in the Winter 1964 *Dissent*.

differences between representative and participatory democracy, or whether it is possible to assert individual freedom in a giant university or bureaucratic labor union. "Let the People Decide," is their semi-mystical slogan.

Finally, the sit-ins were a heroic innovation, fulfilling the students' taste for drama and novelty. Behind the sit-in technique was the pacifist ethic of placing one's body in moral nonviolent confrontation with an existing evil. The Freedom rides, the pilgrimages to Mississippi, the community-organizing projects, are all an extension of this principle of direct moral confrontation.

The eight hundred who sat-in at Sproul Hall in Berkeley, the academics who forged the *teach-in* movement, the teen-agers who *sang-in* for peace at Carnegie Hall last fall—all owe their inspiration to the four Negro freshmen at North Carolina A & T who planted a seed in Greensboro.

In the first weeks the sit-ins spread through the South, Ella Baker was executive secretary of the SCLC, although, as she says now, "just about on my way out." In the 1930's she had worked for the WPA, and in the 1940's she was a field secretary and later director of branches for the NAACP. But during the third week of February she got the idea that some agency had to be created to "provide communication and coordination" among the scores of local sit-in movements.

"It was my idea," Miss Baker said last year, "to call together the leaders of the sit-ins in a small meeting, maybe of about 100, to exchange information and try to find some way of coordinating a spontaneous and unplanned movement."

Miss Baker quickly sold Dr. King on the idea, and the SCLC put up eight hundred dollars for a meeting of student leaders to be held on the Easter weekend of April 15–17. Miss Baker first went to North Carolina A & T, but there was no room on the Greensboro campus for such a large gathering. Next Miss Baker went to Shaw University in Raleigh, from which she had graduated as valedictorian of her class many years before. Her alma mater agreed to host the meeting.

"By the time the meeting was held," Miss Baker recalls, "things had skyrocketed so that 300 people showed up—200 more than we had expected."

From all over the South—even Mississippi—students converged on Raleigh. From Nashville, from Montgomery, from Richmond, and from Pine Bluff they came, by bus and by car and by thumb. And nineteen colleges north of the Mason-Dixon line sent observers. Future leaders of SNCC like Julian Bond, John Lewis, and Ivanhoe Donaldson were there, as was James Bevel, now a top aide to Dr. King.

There was considerable pressure on the young student leaders to affiliate formally with either SCLC or CORE. But almost none of the sit-in activists had had any contact with any adult civil-rights group prior to their demonstrations. The students had an overpowering sense that the sit-ins were *their movement.* After intense debate they decided to maintain "friendly relations" with the SCLC, but to remain independent organizationally. On the last day of the conference the Temporary Student Nonviolent Coordinating Committee was established, and an executive committee, consisting of one person for each of the fifteen different states represented, was set up.

Julian Bond, then a twenty-year-old college student in Atlanta, and now an unseated Georgia legislator, remembers the pressures applied to the students. "People from the SCLC, CORE, the NAACP and every conceivable human relations and civil rights group were at the meeting. Some of them wanted to make the sit-in leaders the nucleus of a youth arm of the SCLC. Others wanted us to become CORE chapters, and the NAACP thought we could raise money for them."

In May the executive committee of fifteen met in Atlanta with Dr. King, Ella Baker, and observers from the National Student Association (NSA), the YMCA, and the American Friends Service Committee. This meeting elected Marion Barry as chairman, decided to open up an office in Atlanta and hire a secretary, to hold another Southwide meeting in October, and to offer testimony to the platform committees of the Democratic and Republican conventions, to be held that summer.

In June, as soon as she graduated from Union Theological Seminary, tiny, white Jane Stembridge came to Atlanta to become office manager for the temporary coordinating group. For two months she worked in a corner of the SCLC office, and later in a small cubicle on Nelson Avenue.

One day, late in June, Bob Parris walked into the office, expecting to be put to work by the SCLC. Ella Baker recalled the incident:

> This quiet soul walked into the office and explained someone in New York had told him there was a job with the SCLC waiting for him in Atlanta. But there had been some foul-up in communication, so we put Bob to work licking envelopes for the student group. He and Jane hit it off immediately, both of them being philosophy students, and they talked about Camus, Tillich and Kant all day. . . . Then we decided to send Bob on a trip through the black belt to find people to attend the October meeting. I guess it was on that trip that he got the idea he should go into Mississippi and try to start a voter registration project.

Also in June of 1960 the first issue of the *Student Voice* was published, and appropriately, amidst the mimeographed news items, there appeared a poem. It was written by twenty-year-old Julian Bond, later to become SNCC's communications director.

> *I, too, hear America singing*
> *But from where I stand*
> *I can only hear Little Richard*
> *and Fats Domino.*

> *But sometimes,*
> *I hear Ray Charles*
> *Drowning in his own tears*
> *or Bird*
> *Relaxing at Camarillo*
> *or Horace Silver doodling*
> *Then I don't mind standing*
> *a little longer*

Through the summer of 1960 the executive committee of this temporary coordinating agency met once a month, in Nashville, in Louisville, and in Jackson, Mississippi. Bond recalls these early meetings this way:

> We really weren't doing very much then. The executive committee would gather and the exchanges would go something like this: "I was arrested four times in the last 30 days, how about you?". . . . "Well, I haven't been arrested, but I've been beaten up twice.". . . "Well, I wasn't arrested or beaten, but I was expelled from school." The meetings were talk sessions and they really didn't accomplish anything. The coordinating committee really didn't do anything until October, when we held our second conference to tighten organizational structure.

SNCC was officially born at the October meeting in Atlanta, a meeting made possible by funds donated by individual Northern students, the Packinghouse Workers' Union, and the SCLC. At this meeting, attended by 235 students and young people, including many from the Black Belt recruited by Parris during the summer, a founding statement of purpose was adopted. It read:

> We affirm the philosophical or religious ideal of non-violence as the foundation of our purpose, the presupposition of our belief, and the manner of our action.

Non-violence, as it grows from the Judeo-Christian tradition, seeks a social order of justice permeated by love. Integration of human endeavor represents the crucial first step towards such a society.

Through non-violence, courage displaces fear. Love transcends hate. Acceptance dissipates prejudice; hope ends despair. Faith reconciles doubt. Peace dominates war. Mutual regards cancel enmity. Justice for all overthrows injustice. The redemptive community supersedes immoral social systems.

By appealing to conscience and standing on the moral nature of human existence, non-violence nurtures the atmosphere in which reconciliation and justice become actual possibilities.

Although each local group in this movement must diligently work out the clear meaning of this statement of purpose, each act or phase of our corporate effort must reflect a genuine spirit of love and good-will.

Within the year SNCC was to be baptized by bombs in southwest Georgia, brutality in Alabama, and murder in Amite County, Mississippi. And phrases like "appealing to conscience" and "genuine spirit of love" began to be replaced by harsher ones like power, politics, and pressure. But until May of 1966, SNCC never abandoned its commitment to nonviolence, made by those first 235 well-dressed middle-class students who met in Atlanta six years ago.

Chapter 4
Amite County

I'm going back out before the rain starts a-falling;
I'll walk to the depths of the deepest dark forest
where the people are many and their hands are all empty
where the pellets of poison are flooding their waters
where the home in the valley meets the damp dirty prison
where the executioner's face is always well hidden
where hunger is ugly, where souls are forgotten
where black is the color, where none is the number

—Bob Dylan

*When you're in Mississippi, the rest of America doesn't seem
real. And when you're in the rest of America, Mississippi doesn't
seem real.*

—Bob Parris

■ In the mythology of the movement, Amite County is a synonym for the Ninth Circle of Hell.

It was to impoverished, remote Amite County, in southwest Mississippi, that SNCC's Bob Parris came in August of 1961 to attempt SNCC's pilot project in voter registration. Beaten twice and jailed thrice, Parris left for the state capital in Jackson after four melancholy months.

It was in Amite that Herbert Lee, a fifty-two-year-old father of nine children, was murdered by E. H. Hurst, a member of the Mississippi state legislature.

It was in Amite that farmer Louis Allen, a witness to Lee's slaying, was shotgunned to death in his home, after he had spoken to the Justice Department about the Lee murder.

It was Amite that saw not a single white volunteer during the 1964 Summer Project because of its legacy of lawlessness.

It was Amite that until July of 1965 had only one registered

Negro voter in the whole county, despite a Negro population majority of 55 percent.

It is Amite that twelve years after Brown v. Board of Education does not have a single classroom desegregated, two years after the 1964 civil rights act does not have a single public facility desegregated, and a year after the 1965 act does not have a federal voting registrar.

It is Amite that has never experienced a civil-rights march, a sit-in, or even a picket line.

It is in rural, red-clayed Amite that the movement has bled itself dry trying to break the century-old trap of terror, poverty, and fear.

Amite is about eighty miles south of Jackson on the Louisiana border. Its county seat is the hamlet of Liberty, population 652.

More than half of the total population of the county is Negro, but only 40 percent of the 13,000 eligible voters are Negro. Because of the hopeless cycle of poverty, many Negroes escape to Baton Rouge, New Orleans, and Chicago while still in their teens. Sociologists have estimated that Negro Emigration from Mississippi is 40 percent. Amite is becoming a place for the very old and the very young.

Although many Negroes in Amite own their own farms, most of them are marginal. Attendance at all-Negro Central High each autumn falls below 50 percent because so many children are required to chop cane and pick cotton on the farms. While this makes the farmer less vulnerable to economic reprisals, it does lead to frequent acts of physical violence.

More than 90 percent of the Negro homes have no heating system or indoor toilet. Only a few have telephones. Almost all rely on hand-dug wells for water. Food must be purchased in Liberty, where Negroes are still beaten up on the street on whim, and where no white has ever stood trial for violence against a Negro.

The sheriff of Amite is six feet, five inch Daniel Jones. His father, Brian Jones, is the Klan leader in the county.

Amite does not have a white, business-oriented middle class that has made Greenville, in the delta, an oasis of decency, or a merchant class that finally, in 1965, helped halt the reign of terror in nearby McComb. It was Hodding Carter's *Greenville Delta-Democrat Times,* and later, Oliver Emmerich's *McComb Enterprise-Journal,* that spread the message of compliance and moderation. The only newspaper in Amite is a racist sheet called the *Liberty Herald.*

Amite seems outside the flow of history, a backward enclave insulated from the passage of time. It has not only missed the civil-rights movement, but the Industrial Revolution as well. There are no factories, no shopping centers, no unions in the county. The longed-for educated, civilized white moderate isn't in hiding; *he doesn't exist in Amite.*

This chapter is an attempt to chronicle the descent of three young Dantes into this one particular hell. This trio of pioneers did not abandon hope, but brought hope to this Ninth Circle.

Liberty is one of the oldest towns in Mississippi, its founding dating back to 1805. Among the earliest settlers in Amite were the poor whites—the "peckerwoods"—who were pushed out of the area around Natchez by the cotton-plantation-owning class of aristocrats. As the South moved toward the Civil War, great tensions developed between the rural peckerwoods of Amite and the affluent, genteel planters of Natchez. When the war began, the residents of Natchez voted to remain in the Union, while the poor whites of Amite chose secession.

After the Civil War, Amite was over 60 percent Negro. There were Negro sheriffs and a powerful Republican Party organization. But after the historic Compromise of 1876 ended Reconstruction, the pattern of Negro disenfranchisement came to Amite, as it did to all of the South. Negroes were lynched, driven off land they owned, beaten, and their right to vote taken away. Most Negroes who own their own land in Amite today do so only because one of their ancestors fought for it with guns or fists.

Most of the Amite Negroes, however, fled to the rich soil of the delta, where cheap labor was needed to clear the swamps for the future plantations.

The diminution of Negro power in the county has continued all through the twentieth century. The only Negro resistance to this trend came during the 1930's when several of Huey Long's Share the Wealth Leagues sprang up in the area, but they were violently suppressed. The remote rurality and the backward poverty of Amite have been the jaws of the vise that has bled the Amite Negro since Reconstruction.

Robert Parris Moses grew up in a housing project on the edge of Harlem. But somehow he was not swallowed up by the squalor and violence of the ghetto like so many of his contemporaries. Instead, gifted with a philosophical and poetic mind, he went downtown at age thirteen, as a result of high grades on a competitive examination, to virtually all-white, academically superior, Stuyvesant High School. There Parris not only compiled outstanding grades, but was captain of Stuyvesant's championship basketball quintet, and vice president of his graduating class.

Parris then went, on a scholarship, to predominantly white Hamilton College in Clinton, New York, where again he excelled in both scholarship and sports. It was at Hamilton that a French instructor introduced him to the writings of Albert Camus, whose melancholy morality was to make a lasting impact on his thinking. Almost a decade later, addressing volunteers at Oxford, Ohio, for the Mississippi Summer Project, Parris compared racism to Camus's plague, and the volunteers to the sanitary squads.

From Hamilton, Parris went on to graduate school at Harvard, and received a master's degree in philosophy in 1957. Afterward Parris began to teach math at one of New York City's elite private schools—Horace Mann, in the Riverdale section of the Bronx. Nothing in his first twenty-four years—spent increasingly in the white world—seemed to indicate that Parris was destined to become a myth-shrouded legend to thousands of young radicals, and to have his picture hang in a sharecropper shack in the delta next to Abraham Lincoln's and John F. Kennedy's.

Folk singer Bob Cohen, who lived with Parris in Manhattan from September of 1960 until he left for Amite in July of 1961, remembers him as "extraordinarily quiet, gentle, abstract . . . really involved with his students and reading a lot—Bertrand Russell and Camus in French. . . . Yet, I always had the sense he was very busy in his head all the time."

Cohen met Parris at the Maine Folk Dance Camp in June of 1960, and recalls, "One of the few times I can remember Bob's face really lit up was when he was folk dancing. He loved it. I remember sometimes we would be coming home late from a party or something, and if Bob had had a good time, he would start dancing down Amsterdam Avenue. He could be very free and gay then."

Cohen, who named his first child after his roommate, says, "Bob hardly ever talked about going back South after his trip in June of 1960. . . . The only hint I got of the deep feeling he had about going back South was that he would sit for hours and listen to a record of Odetta singing, 'I'm Going Back to the Red Clay Country.' "

Nineteen hundred and sixty-one, when Parris went back to the red clay of Amite and Pike counties, marked the first time a SNCC worker tried to live in and become part of a community. It was the first time SNCC engaged in voter registration. It was probably the most creative and heroic single act anyone in the New Left has attempted. Certainly much of the subsequent history of the New Left has flowed from that existential act of Parris disappearing alone into the most violent and desolate section of Mississippi.

As a consequence of that deed and his own selfless personality, Parris occupies a legendary niche in the New Left. He has been compared to Danilo Dolci, Hesse's Siddhartha, and Prince Kropotkin. Perhaps the reverential feeling about this shy, often sad prophet was best expressed by Dick Gregory when he introduced

Parris to the mammoth Berkeley teach-in in May of 1965 with these words:

> I refused to do my act a few minutes ago because it was too light. Now it's dark enough, but I looked over my shoulder and found some light that I must get rid of first. This is a young man who has done more for my life without even knowing it to make me commit my life for right over wrong. Thank goodness I happened to be in the right place at the right time when he was speaking in his own little way. Many times I listened to him when he thought I was asleep in jail; many times I overheard him in the sharecropping fields of Mississippi. I'd like to postpone my act for another few minutes and bring to the stand a man who to me and to many people, will stand up among the greatest human beings who have ever walked the face of the earth. I don't have to say any more. I would like to present to you a *man*—Bob Parris.

The series of events that propelled Parris into the Ninth Circle of Amite began during the summer of 1960. It was then that Parris, while traveling through Mississippi trying to recruit Negro students to attend SNCC's October founding conference, met Amzie Moore, the indomitable leader of the NAACP chapter in Cleveland, Mississippi. In the course of several conversations Moore convinced the twenty-five-year-old SNCC field secretary he should quit his teaching job and return to the delta the following summer to begin a voter-registration campaign. Parris agreed, and in November the popular Negro magazine, *Jet*, printed a short item describing the projected venture. Amite County's NAACP founder and leader, E. W. Steptoe, saw the *Jet* item, and along with Pike County leader C. C. Bryant, wrote a letter to Parris in New York, suggesting he change his plans and try to organize a project in southwest Mississippi. At that point only 38 of 9,000 Pike County Negroes were registered to vote, and one of

5,500 in Amite was eligible to vote, according to Civil Rights Commission figures.

Parris, who was encountering unexpected difficulty in finding a church willing to house a voter-registration school in the delta, agreed to come to the Amite-Pike region.

Civil-rights workers had not even tried to enter Mississippi until 1952. According to Elizabeth Sutherland, in her *Letters from Mississippi*, the "first 'agitator' was shot and killed, the second was shot and run out of the state." Next came Bob Parris in July, of 1961, without a grand scheme, lacking any concrete experience in voter registration.

On August 7th the SNCC Pike County voter-registration school opened up in a hamlet called Burglundtown in a two-story structure, which included a grocery below and a Masonic meeting hall above. The only teacher was Parris, and the student body consisted of about 20 Negroes, half of them too young to vote.

After the first class four persons went to the registrar's office in nearby Magnolia, the county seat, and three of them registered without incident. Three Negroes went down on August 9th, and two registered successfully. Nine journeyed to Magnolia on August 10th, and one was registered. The next night one of the Pike County Negroes who had attempted to register was shot at by a white farmer. The next day only two people showed up at the voter-registration school.

Parris then went into Amite, living on Steptoe's farm. On August 15th, he accompanied an old farmer named Ernest Isaac and two middle-aged women, Bertha Lee Hughes and Matilda Schoby, to the courthouse in Liberty. The trio managed to fill out a form, but not to take the test. As they were driving out of Liberty, toward McComb, their car was flagged down by a highway patrolman, who told Isaac, the driver, to get out and come into the police car. Isaac quickly complied, but Parris also got out of the car and asked the officer why. He was pushed and ordered back into the car. At that point the patrolman arrested Parris for "impeding an officer in the discharge of his duties." Taken to McComb, Parris was fined fifty dollars, and for the first of many times saw the inside of a Mississippi jail, as he spent two days in prison, fasting, rather than pay the fine.

On Monday, August 28th, Parris started a voter-registration class at Mt. Pilgrim Church, the first in the history of Amite County. The next day he went with Reverend Alfred Knox and Curtis Dawson to the courthouse in Liberty to try to register. A block from the courthouse they were met by Billy Jack Caston, a cousin of the sheriff and the son-in-law of state representative E. H. Hurst. Without saying a word, Caston walked up to Parris and knocked him down with a punch to the temple. He then proceeded to pummel Parris for several minutes with punches to the head and ribs. Parris just sat in the street trying to protect himself as best he could in the traditional nonviolent position, his head between his knees and his arms shielding his face. Reverend Knox tried to pull Caston off his victim, but white bystanders ordered him not to intervene.

Knox and Dawson never made it to the courthouse. Instead they picked up the semiconscious Parris and drove him to Steptoe's farm. Steptoe later recalled, "I didn't recognize Bob at first he was so bloody. I just took off his tee-shirt and wrung out the blood like it had just been washed." Then Steptoe drove Parris to a Negro doctor in McComb, who took eight stitches in his scalp.

The next day Amite experienced another first: Parris filed assault and battery charges against Caston, the first time in that area a Negro had challenged the right of a white man to beat him up at will. The warrant was made out by the county district attorney after the county judge refused.

The trial was held in the Liberty courthouse on August 31st. More than 100 whites, many of them openly armed, jammed the courtroom for the spectacle. While on the stand, Parris was asked by Caston's attorney whether he had participated in riots the year before in Japan or San Francisco. After his testimony Parris—the plaintiff—was told by the sheriff he had better leave the courtroom because he could not guarantee his safety. So before the trial ended in Caston's acquittal, Parris was given a police escort to the Pike County line.

Meanwhile, two other crucial events were happening during the month of August. One was a SNCC staff meeting at the Highlander Folk School in Tennessee. At that meeting the fledgling organization was divided into two camps, one favoring direct action on the order of the sit-ins and the freedom rides, and the other suggesting the innovation of voter registration. Hints from the Kennedy Administration that it would look favorably on voter-registration activities, plus financial support from the New World and other foundations, strengthened the voter-registration group in SNCC. After prolonged debate, SNCC decided to adopt "an all-out revolutionary program encompassing both mass direct action and voter registration drives."

The second thing to happen during August was the gradual emergence from jail in Jackson of the first group of freedom riders. Four of these freedom riders, Reggie Robinson of Baltimore, John Hardy of Nashville, Travis Britt of New York, and MacArthur Cotton of Jackson, were to join Parris before the month was over. Also, direct-action partisans like Marion Barry came to McComb during August and sparked a series of sit-ins and protest marches. A fifteen-year-old McComb high-school student, Brenda Travis, and five friends sat-in and were arrested. Her companions were sentenced to eight months for "breach of the peace," and Brenda was turned over to juvenile authorities and sentenced to one year in the state school for delinquents. Later, more than 100 of Brenda's classmates at Burgland High School marched through McComb to protest her severe sentence and expulsion from school. They were all arrested as they knelt praying at the steps of the city hall.

More violence in Liberty.

On September 5th, Parris and Travis Britt accompanied four Negroes to the courthouse. In his pamphlet, *Revolution in Missis-*

sippi, Tom Hayden recorded Britt's terse description of the events that followed:

There was a clerk directly across the hall who came rushing out while we were waiting, and ordered us to leave the hallway. He said he didn't want a bunch of people congregating in the hallway. So we left and walked around the building to the courthouse, near the registrar's window. By the time we reached the back of the building a group of white men had filed into the hall. . . . They were talking belligerently. Finally one of the white men came to the end of the hall as if looking for someone. He asked us if we knew Mr. Brown. We said no. He said, you boys must not be from around here. We said he was correct. This conversation was interrupted by another white man who approached Bob Moses (Parris) and started preaching to him: how he should be ashamed of coming down here from New York stirring up trouble, causing poor innocent people to lose their homes and jobs, and how he (Bob) was lower than dirt on the ground for doing such things, and how he should get down on his knees and ask God forgiveness for every sin in his lifetime. Bob asked him why the people should lose their homes just because they wanted to register and vote. The white gentleman did not answer the question, but continued to preach. He said that the Negro men were raping the white women up North, and that he wouldn't allow such a thing to start down here in Mississippi. . . . At this point Bob turned away and sat on the stoop of the courthouse porch, and the man talking to him took a squatting position. Nobody was saying anything. I reached into my pocket and took out a cigarette. A tall white man, about middle-aged, wearing a khaki shirt and pants stepped up to me and asked, "Boy, what's your business?" at which point I knew I was in trouble. The clerk from the hallway came to the backdoor leading to the courthouse with a smile on his face and called to the white man, "Wait a minute, wait a minute!" At this point the white man, who they called Bryant, hit me on my right eye. Then I saw this clerk motion his head as if to call the rest of the whites. They came and all circled around me, and this fellow that was called Bryant hit me on my jaw and then on my chin. Then he slammed me down; instead of falling I stumbled onto the courthouse lawn. The crowd (about 15, I think) followed, making comments. He was holding me so tight around the collar, I put my hands on my collar to ease the choking. This set off a reaction of punches from this fellow they called Bryant; I counted fifteen; he just kept hitting and shouting, "Why don't you hit me, nigger?" I was beaten into a semi-conscious state. My vision was blurred by the punch to the eye. I heard Bob yell to cover my head to avoid any further blows to my face. . . . Bob took me by the arm and took me to the street, walking cautiously to avoid any further kicks or blows. The Negro fellow that had been taking the registration test gave up in the excitement, and we saw him in his truck. . . .

This incident, in the heart of the hell Bob Parris says isn't real unless you're there, went unreported in the national press. This was still three years before the Summer Project, and such beatings administered to blacks were so commonplace as not to fit the definition of news. Such beatings, however, turned out to have considerable news content in 1964, when the bloodied recipients were white students from "good families" in the North. In 1961 the blood of Parris and Britt was invisible.

The beating had its desired effect. Attendance at meetings and voter-registration classes dwindled to almost nothing. The small group of SNCC workers walked the back roads from dawn to dusk in a vain search for Negroes willing to try to register in Liberty. "But the farmers were no longer willing to go down," Parris later recalled, "and for the rest of the month of September we just had a rough time."

Amite's unchecked, legally sanctioned violence became murder on September 25th, when Herbert Lee was shot to death in front of the Liberty cotton gin by E. H. Hurst.

The day before, Parris had met with Steptoe and John Doar of the Justice Department at Steptoe's farm. Steptoe had told Doar that Hurst, whose land is adjacent to his, had publicly threatened to kill him and Herbert Lee. Lee had attended voter-registration classes and had volunteered a few days before to attempt to register in Liberty, the first individual to do so since the beating of Britt.

Lee was shot once in the brain by Hurst's .38 caliber revolver. It happened about noon in front of a dozen witnesses, including several Negroes. Lee, wearing his farmer's overalls and field boots, was sitting in the cab of his pick-up truck, and fell out into the gutter when he was shot. For two hours his body lay in a pool of blood, uncovered and swarmed over by insects. Finally, a coroner from McComb came and picked it up. That same afternoon a coroner's jury in Liberty met, and ruled that Lee was killed in self-defense.

Parris felt responsible for Lee's death, just as three years later he was to feel himself responsible for the deaths of Goodman, Chaney, and Schwerner. For the next three nights, from sundown till almost sunup, he walked and rode through the mist-shrouded rolling hills of Amite, knocking on strange doors, seeking the three Negro witnesses. Fighting off exhaustion, waking up families that had to get up at 5 A.M., Parris finally found the Negro farmers who had witnessed the slaying. But none was willing to tell a grand jury the truth. Instead they told Parris that the sheriff and deputy sheriff had warned them to tell everyone that Lee, who was about five feet four, had tried to hit Hurst, who is six feet three, with a tire iron.

One of the three witnesses was a farmer named Louis Allen. Late in October a federal grand jury convened to consider an indictment of Hurst. It was then that Allen drove to McComb to inform Parris he had changed his mind, and would tell the truth about Lee's death if he was guaranteed federal protection.

Parris called the Justice Department in Washington but was told it was "impossible" to provide Allen with protection. So Allen testified to the federal jury that Hurst had killed Lee in self-protection. Six months later a deputy sheriff told Allen he knew he had contacted the Justice Department, and he broke Allen's jaw with a flashlight. On January 31, 1964, Allen was found dead on his front porch as a result of three shotgun blasts.

Tormented by the shadows of guilt, Parris has tried to make Herbert Lee a symbol for all the hundreds of Mississippi Negroes who have been lawlessly murdered by whites. Whenever he spoke in the North in 1962 or 1963 he would talk about Herbert Lee, and soon thousands of young people knew of this one murder out of many. Lee was also memorialized in a song, "Never Turn Back," written in 1963 by Bertha Gober, a wide-eyed teen-ager from Albany, Georgia. For a while the song, a dirge sung at a slow, elegiac tempo, was the "We Shall Overcome" of the SNCC workers in Mississippi. Its final verse goes:

> *We have hung our heads and cried*
> *Cried for those like Lee who died*
> *Died for you and died for me*
> *Died for the cause of equality*
> *No, we'll never turn back*
> *No, we'll never turn back*
> *Until we've all been freed*
> *And we have equality*
> *And we have equality*

The murder of Lee broke the back of whatever had been stirring in Amite. Few Negroes were willing to be seen talking to Parris or to the other "freedom riders," as they were called by both Negroes and whites. The tiny flicker of hope from Parris' candle went out, and Amite's Negroes were left to curse the darkness.

A month later Parris went to jail for two months in Pike County for leading a march of 118 high-school students to the McComb city hall. From the Magnolia jail he smuggled out a note to the SNCC office in Atlanta. The last few paragraphs illuminate Parris' speculative and poetic turn of mind.

> Later on, Hollis [Hollis Watkins, now a member of SNCC's executive committee] will lead out with a clear tenor into a freedom song, Talbert and Lewis will supply jokes, and McDew [Chuck McDew, then SNCC's chairman] will discourse on the history of the black man and the Jew. McDew—a black by birth and a Jew by choice, and a revolutionary by necessity—has taken on the deep loves and the deep hates which America, and the world, reserve for those who dare to stand in a strong sun and cast a sharp shadow.
>
> In the words of Judge Brumfield, who sentenced us, we are "cold calculators" who design to disrupt the racial harmony (harmonious since 1619) of McComb into racial strife and rioting; we, he said, are the leaders who are causing young children to be led like sheep to the pen and be slaughtered (in a legal manner). "Robert," he was addressing me, "haven't some of the people from your school been able to go down and register without violence here in Pike County?" I thought to myself that Southerners are most exposed when they boast. . . .
>
> This is Mississippi, in the middle of the iceberg. Hollis is leading off with his tenor, "Michael row the boat ashore, Alleluia; Christian brothers don't be slow, Alleluia; Mississippi's next to go, Alleluia." This is a tremor in the middle of the iceberg—from a stone that the builders rejected.

In January Parris left southwest Mississippi, melancholy and depressed, to begin a pilgrimage that was to lead to the Mississippi

Summer Project, the Freedom Democratic Party, and a 100 percent rise in Negro registration in the state by the end of 1965 (25,000 to 50,000).

But for three years Amite was to remain that base of the iceberg most submerged beneath the ocean of terror. Nobody tried to register in Liberty after the murder of Herbert Lee. No SNCC project was attempted in the county. No summer volunteer was sent into the hills and woods of Amite. For three years a pattern of life incomprehensible to an outsider endured without assault. Negroes were beaten and killed. Whites, a minority of the county, continued to make every political and economic decision. No word was written about the iceberg, and the tiny crack Parris had made froze over.

E. W. Steptoe, a small, reedlike man with a time-trampled face, has lived in Amite all his fifty-six years. He was there trying to register before Parris came; he was there after Parris moved on to Jackson and Greenwood; and he is there today, shaming, cajoling, bullying Negroes into registering.

Steptoe is not a saint. He is a violent man and an egotistical one. He can be demagogic at meetings, and he can con reporters and naïve visitors. But there are few men like him in the whole state of Mississippi. His courage, his common-sense wisdom, his bittersweet wit and love, are the special qualities of the rural Mississippi Negro, who lives by his wits to survive, and whose life depends on human bonds with others.

Steptoe first tried to register in 1953 and was told he flunked the test. In 1954, after reading about the Supreme Court's desegregation decision, he organized an Amite County chapter of the NAACP. Its third meeting, however, was broken up by armed Klansmen with the help of the deputy sheriff.

"My uncle was so scared after that meeting," Steptoe recalls, "he ran into the woods and stayed there for a week, living on raw food. Then he finally came out and left the county."

In June of 1964 Amite sheriff Daniel Jones visited a score of

Negro homes, making it clear there would be reprisals if they put up white summer volunteers. Steptoe was the only Negro in the county who said he would house "as many white civil rights workers that will fit in my house." The final decision not to send any volunteers to Amite County was made in Jackson after Goodman, Chaney, and Schwerner were reported missing in Neshoba County.

One of the 650 summer volunteers was a rabbi's son from Bakersfield, California, named Marshall Ganz. During the summer Ganz worked in McComb on one of the more effective SNCC projects, along with Curtis Hayes, Mendy Samstein, J. D. Smith, and Dennis Sweeney. Their freedom house was bombed in August, and Hayes narrowly escaped death. At the end of the summer Ganz was one of the 150 who chose to remain.

Elizabeth Sutherland remembers the first time she met Ganz in July of 1964:

As soon as I saw him I knew he would be one of those volunteers who would stay in the state. Marshall seemed more mature and more sophisticated than most of the other volunteers. He was an economic radical, but more important, he had a sensitive, literary kind of mind. He was the type of person who was driven to become part of people's lives in a deep way. He seemed more concerned with human relationships than with staging big demonstrations. I think Marshall could be a fine novelist if he ever had the time to reflect on his experiences.

So in January of 1965 Ganz moved to Steptoe's farm to become the first full-time SNCC worker since Parris in Amite County. Miss Sutherland now suspects it was Ganz' "passion for human contact" that led him to abandon the "impersonalization of a city like McComb, to live directly with the poor farmers in Amite."

In McComb, Ganz had lived in a freedom house with about 10

other staff members, and had been somewhat removed from the rhythm of life in the Negro community. But at Steptoe's farm he was at the vortex of it, and intimately involved in people's everyday life.

For six months Ganz canvassed alone in Amite; tedious, repetitive, frustrating drudgery. Hour after hour, day after day, he would walk the deserted gravel roads of the county, talking, visiting, joking with people who had never seen a friendly white face before in their lives. For six months all he did was try to find local Negroes who were willing to act against the system that emasculated them.

Early in July two more SNCC staff members—both girls— joined Ganz and Steptoe in Amite. One was twenty-year-old Hazel Lee, a Negro from Panola County and a veteran of six arrests and a hundred picket lines. Hazel came, she says, "because I heard that Amite was a really tough place where there had been a lot of killings. I felt I had to go there."

The other was a Jewish girl from Brooklyn named Carol Rogoff, a 1963 graduate of Beaver College near Philadelphia. Carol did not come to fashionable Beaver a rebel. But during the summer of 1963 she became active in the SNCC-ignited movement in Cambridge, Maryland. She was almost expelled from college, and there were tensions with her conservative family, but she continued to work in the movement after the summer in Cambridge.

In 1965 Carol was in charge of organizing high-school students in New York City. During the Easter vacation she escorted a group of those students on a visit to McComb, repaying a trip made by a group of McComb students to New York the previous Christmas. While in McComb, Carol made a few trips to Steptoe's farm, and was so touched by the pure, slow movement being built in Amite she decided to return there as a SNCC field secretary in July.

Ganz, Rogoff, and Lee were all part of the SNCC faction most committed to decentralization and grass-roots decision-making, and most antagonistic to flashy demonstrations and leader-oriented mass rallies. All agreed the movement in Amite must be built slowly and with care, from the bottom up.

"A big influx of volunteers would smother the movement here," said Carol, "as it did in McComb. If anything is to be built in Amite it must be inward, rather than outside-oriented. What has to be done is to build a community of local people who trust each other and are willing to act on their grievances; local Negroes who are willing to take responsibility and make decisions democratically."

After weeks of canvassing and church meetings of thirty and forty people, it was finally decided a group of Negroes would try to register on July 22nd at the Liberty courthouse. By then the voting rights act was about to be signed by the President, and the Mississippi legislature had passed a new law liberalizing the procedures for voter registration, to prevent application of the federal law to Mississippi. Marshall Ganz called the Justice Department in Washington and the FBI in McComb to inform them of the registration bid, but in order to thwart dependence on whites, none of the SNCC workers accompanied the twenty-two Amite Negroes to Liberty on July 22nd.

At 9 A.M. they were lined up outside the courthouse, only a few yards from the spot where Herbert Lee's body had lain for two hours. The group included Steptoe, making his eighth attempt to register; Reverend Knox, who had made that first bloody trip to Liberty with Bob Parris in 1961; Ben Faust, a seventy-seven-year-old farmer who once spent five years in the infamous Parchman Prison for allegedly stealing a cow; and William Weathersby, a militant farmer who had attended registration classes in 1961.

"Okay, who's first?" asked Sheriff Jones, his hand ominously fingering his gun.

Silence.

Then William Sibley, a farmer, stepped forward and announced, "Me."

By dusk all twenty-two had been registered to vote.

A month later about 200 Negroes were registered, including the widow of Herbert Lee and one of his nine children.

All summer Ganz, Rogoff, and Lee worked hard, winning slowly the confidence of the community, then its respect, and finally, its love. When they ate, it was a meal forced on them by the community, by those who had less than enough to feed their own families. Local whites began to spread dozens of nails each night in Steptoe's gravel driveway, and the project's one beat-up car suffered from a series of flat tires. The car was a necessity in the completely rural county, and calls would go out in the middle of the night to friends in New York and California, asking for money needed to fix the flats so that as few days as possible would be wasted.

In September Marshall left Amite, planning to return after a few months' rest, perhaps with a tape recorder to document the saga of the Ninth Circle. But instead, Marshall went to California to help in the dramatic grape-pickers' strike near Delano. He quickly involved other SNCC workers in the strike and became a close aide to strike leader Cesar Chavez, whom *The New Republic*'s Andrew Kopkind has compared to Bob Parris.

In November I visited Amite.

As one drives from Jackson to Amite along fog-clouded Highway 51, the abstract sociological term "rural" becomes concretized. The sense of desolation and backwardness grows with each mile on the speedometer. There are no cities except for McComb, whose thirteen thousand inhabitants make it a metropolis by Mississippi standards. Next to Jackson, the capital, the biggest city in the state is Meridian, population fifty thousand. Perhaps one of the reasons for Mississippi's primitive racism is the absence of a cultured urban center that might civilize the population from within. Georgia has Atlanta, Louisiana has New Orleans, even Alabama has Montgomery. But

Mississippi has Meridian, where the killers of Goodman, Chaney, and Schwerner are still free.

Even a short stay in Amite is a bruising experience. Old Negroes with bent spines and work-swollen fingers lie to the SNCC workers, inventing ailments and appointments, rather than face the local registrar in Liberty. A meeting in a broken-down shack called a church approaches Gandhian *agape* with the singing of religious hymns and the preachments of love thy enemy. A home with no toilet, no telephone, and no heat, and with six children crowded into three small rooms, is spotlessly clean, and a magnificent meal is prepared for a dozen people in two hours. An old farmer named Willie Bates recalls how his cousin was castrated in 1962 and asks whether "there is any place on earth where colored peoples is treated meaner than in Amite County?"

Fear and Love.

These are the two polarities upon which the fragile, embryonic movement in Amite rests.

The movement in Amite is in an earlier stage than anywhere else in Mississippi. Even the most rebellious local Negroes think a public demonstration in Liberty must wait for another age. The protest in Amite is pure and religious, uncontaminated by organizational in-fighting or Mau Mau militancy. It is just two outside organizers and perhaps 200 or 300 local Negroes. The *right* to protest has not yet been won, much less the tokens of desegregation or the utopian goal of equality. For a Negro to talk to another Negro active in the movement requires courage; to come to a meeting is authentic heroism. There is not much talk about Herbert Lee, but there is a lot of remembering.

The daily routine of Steptoe, Carol, and Hazel is "boring, shitty" work, as Carol puts it. It is canvassing from sunup until twilight, and then often a meeting in a church. There is nothing dramatic about the work. There are no emotional releases. The tension is constant: every passing car is a threat, every white face a mask for violence, every back road a potential trap. There is no freedom house in Amite, where drink, talk, or sex can be shared with other organizers. There is nothing more intellectual than the *McComb Enterprise-Journal* to read. By November both Carol and Hazel had been there for five months and both were preparing to leave, burned-out by the tension, the exhaustion, the frustration, of day-to-day work.

Religion is the source of love in Amite. Baptist churches are the only possible places to hold meetings. Several of the indigenous leaders developing in Amite, like Reverend Knox, are ministers, or, at least, deacons in their church, like Curtis Dawson. The people themselves are deeply religious.

There is no tradition of freedom singing in Amite. Few Negroes even know the words to "We Shall Overcome." The four meetings I attended while in the county were all begun with the singing of Baptist hymns and a prayer. There were none of the fiery call-and-response chants of "Freedom now" or of the improvised freedom songs that characterize the movement in urban centers.

One of the meetings I attended was in Mt. Pilgrim Baptist Church on Steptoe's land, where Parris had conducted his first voter-registration class in 1961. Herbert Lee is buried in the churchyard, and his handsome fifteen-year-old son, Herbert Jr., was among the fifty people present at the meeting.

Mt. Pilgrim has no pulpit. There are just ten rows of spare wooden benches in the center, and four rows on either side. It is lighted by only three bulbs. Outside it was 45 degrees, and until the warmth from the small heater spread throughout the room, few people took off their jackets. A hand-drawn tablet with the Ten Commandments was on the wall.

One by one, individuals began drifting in, some in blue denim field overalls and mud-caked boots, others in sports jackets and shirts open at the neck. The men and women segregated themselves by sex.

The meeting began with the singing of two hymns: "Lord,

Come By Here," and "Jesus, Hold My Hand While I Run This Race." Then there was a prayer by Reverend A. D. Hackett, an itinerant preacher without a permanent church. "God is going to cure our troubles through somebody," he said in a prophecy that synthesized the Bible with the movement.

I had come to Amite with young folk singer Eric Andersen. We, along with Carol, were the only whites at the meeting, and Steptoe used our faces as his text for the evening. (Steptoe is one of the few local Negroes who is not religious.)

"White people come down here and do everything for us," he began. "But you have to do just one thing for them—and that's to redish."

Chants of "Amen," and "That's right," welled up from the benches.

"We're going through something here now that should have happened years ago. I've been in this struggle since 1953 and now I can see the first change happening."

More amens greeted that affirmative observation.

"You all have to go down and redish now. You should want to make this a better county to live in. You have to take that first step. You get the key to freedom when you redish. To be a re-dished *voter* means you are an American, a first-class citizen. It will keep bullets out of your body and clubs away from your head."

Curtis Dawson, with a morose, bespectacled face, not unlike Bob Parris', spoke in the same vein of civic virtue and racial reconciliation. It was a sermon of love no Harlem hustler could comprehend.

"We must love everybody," he started.

From that opening statement he began to build, the way a blues singer states, restates, and then embroiders on a basic theme.

"White people care more about us than we care about ourselves," Deacon Dawson added, the counterpoint of amens and "Say it, brother," rising from the benches.

"They do everything for us. They go farther with us than we go with ourselves. But we have to redish for our own selves."

With that, the amens swelled up again.

And then, as is often done in Amite, a political point was cloaked in a biblical analogy.

"God told Moses," Dawson said, "to pick up a stick. But Moses said it was a snake. But the Lord insisted he pick it up, and when Moses did, it turned out to be a sword. And that's how going to the courthouse in Liberty seems. Right now it looks like picking up a snake. But once you pick it up, it will become the sword of freedom."

Then Carol Rogoff, sitting in the last row, began to sing, "This Little Light of Mine." And the younger people in the church, some of whom had gone to jail in Jackson in June, joined in, and Eric Andersen began to contribute a guitar accompaniment.

"This little light of mine/we're gonna let it shine. . . ."

The words filled the church and spilled out into the frosty night. With modulating fervor, each new chorus was sung.

"All over Mississippi, we're gonna let it shine. . . .

"All over the courthouse, we're gonna let it shine. . . .

"All over Sheriff Jones, we're gonna let it shine. . . .

"All over the highway, we're gonna let it shine. . . .

"All over Liberty, we're gonna let it shine/oh, we've got the light of freedom/we're gonna let it shine."

Most of the older people had left, since Amite farmers must get up at 5 A.M. But a cluster of teen-agers remained around Eric, singing the songs they had learned in jail.

After a while Herbert Lee, Jr., began to sing:

"Oh, my father was a freedom fighter/I'm a freedom fighter too. . . ."

Fear.

That's the other emotion always just beneath the surface of life in Amite. It is there whenever you stop for gas in Liberty; whenever the dogs start barking in the night and someone is approaching the house; whenever you notice the gun Steptoe always keeps within reach.

One incident that happened to me helped demonstrate the total vulnerability of Amite Negroes to random violence. Four of us—Carol, Hazel, a local woman named Juanitta Griffin, and I—were nailing up posters on trees for the Agricultural Stabilization and Conservation election. The ASC county committees decide local cotton allotments, who gets extra acreage, and who gets community credit corporation loans. Until Carol and Hazel came to work in Amite, Negro farmers didn't know they were eligible to run in this election even if they weren't registered to vote in political elections. The Federal Government hadn't bothered to inform them of their right to participate.

I had just nailed a poster to a tree and we were driving away when we noticed a pick-up truck stop and the driver tear down the poster. For about a quarter of a mile the truck followed us on the deserted, narrow gravel road. We noticed it had no license plate. The driver had a woman, a child, and a Negro in the cab with him. Suddenly he came up on us very fast, trying to drive us off the road. He barely missed. He drove on a few hundred yards to discharge his three passengers. Then he began to come up on us again from behind, making a second pass, again coming very close to forcing us off the road. By this time we were growing frightened, realizing that we didn't know where we were and that the driver of the tagless pick-up truck had us at his mercy.

Carol, who was driving, suggested we try to make it to a paved road less than a mile away. Just then the pick-up truck bore down on us, head-on, at about 60 miles an hour. Carol swerved, and our car landed in a ditch.

We were destroying all the lists of local Negroes we had in the car when the driver of the pick-up truck pulled up alongside. He had a face from central casting, like all the faces I had watched in newsreels spitting on little girls in Little Rock and unleashing snarling police dogs in Birmingham.

"You-all need any help?" he asked mockingly.

"No, thank you," Carol replied.

"Well, if you-all did, I'd tell you-all to call Martin Luther," the face said, and drove off to a dairy barn up the road.

The four of us quickly got out and began to walk as fast as we could in the direction of the main road. As we walked past the dairy barn, the driver, now with a friend and a pack of dogs, began shouting at us.

"White trash . . . nigger lovers . . . degenerates. . . ."

We kept walking, heads down, and he began following us, cursing and threatening.

Before he caught up to us we reached the main road and flagged down a log truck with three Negroes. But the Negroes were afraid to pick up our integrated group. Only several minutes of pleading convinced them to take us to a nearby home, where Carol called FBI agent R. L. Timmons, stationed in McComb.

Agent Timmons said he was busy just then, but would come to Steptoe's farm the next morning to hear our stories.

Within a few hours the grapevine in the Negro community reported back that the man who had chased us was named Dan "Buster" Wells, and that he had a long history of brutality against Negroes. The Negro originally in the truck with Wells was also spoken to, but he wouldn't talk to us, much less to the FBI. The Negroes in Amite remember Louis Allen, too.

The next morning Agent Timmons arrived exactly on time, wearing a businessman's blue suit. He carefully took down all our statements, but added he didn't think "anything would come of them."

"We don't have any jurisdiction," he said, incanting the phrase that has made FBI agents despised by civil-rights workers. "Why didn't you call Sheriff Jones when this happened?" he asked.

Carol reminded Agent Timmons that many local Negroes believed that Sheriff Jones had personally murdered Louis Allen, and that he had never arrested a white man for violence against a Negro.

The next day, on the street in McComb, we accidentally ran into Timmons' assistant, Sy Hoglund. While Timmons grew up in Louisiana and is clearly hostile to the movement, Hoglund is a northerner who went to law school at the University of Wisconsin. He reluctantly admitted that since we were working on the federal ASC election when the incident occurred, "there might be jurisdiction . . . but we will not do anything more than file a report unless the Justice Department specifically instructs us to proceed further in the case."

Bob Parris, Marshall Ganz, and Carol Rogoff are all complex, city-bred, middle-class intellectuals. That Amite should attract and sustain such people is, I suspect, an insight into one of the New Left's most tangled threads. That thread is the revolt against the IBM card, against urban impersonalization and the alienation of mass society; a revolt rooted in the void, which cries out for the kind of human generosity and vitality that exists among rural Mississippi Negroes.

Many civil-rights workers in the state rage passionately against the life-style they left behind in the comfortable North: suburbia, status commodities, nine-to-five jobs. But in Amite people are judged not by their manners, or their fathers' income, or what fraternity they belong to, but by their integrity, their work, and their courage.

Although it is too often sentimentalized, there is a special quality to the Negroes of Amite County that is missing elsewhere. The routinized middle class doesn't have it, the cynical Northern-ghetto Negro doesn't have it, and the violent, poor Southern white doesn't have it. In part this distinctive quality comes from living in a totally rural environment, removed from the criminality, corruption, and violence in the cities. In part it derives from the strength of the Baptist Church with its embracing of the values of both the Sermon on the Mount and the Ten Commandments. And in part it comes from a people that has achieved an authentic nobility in one hundred years of stoic suffering.

In *Letters from Mississippi*, a few of the volunteers reached for an explanation for their love of a culture they had been taught, in America's best schools, was slow and primitive.

"One sees freedom here," one volunteer wrote, "that is so much more than the ironical fact that enslaved people are, at least relatively, the liberated ones. Some 'white' people sit at their feet wondering at this sorrow freed and made beautiful. . . ."

Another summer worker wrote home: "When I see these simple people living lives of relative inner peace, love, honor, courage and humor, I lose patience with people who sit and ponder their belly buttons. . . ."

Still another volunteer observed: "There is some strong ambivalence which goes with this work. I sometimes fear that I am only helping to integrate some beautiful people into modern white society with all of its depersonalization (I suppose that has something to do with its industrial nature). It isn't 19th century pastoral romanticism which I feel, but a genuine respect and admiration for a culture which, for all the trouble, still isn't as commercialized and depersonalized as our Northern mass culture."

What I am trying to suggest is the ultimate irony of the New Left's assault on the Closed Society. It is that the liberators have so far benefited more from the struggle than those in bondage, that for all the enormity of their heroism, Parris, Ganz, and Rogoff have gotten more than they have given. And it may be an enduring paradox that all through Mississippi the lives of the white volunteers have been more enriched, and more fundamentally changed, than the lives of the maids and tenant farmers whom they came to help.

Such a tentative suggestion, finally, flows from a suffocating pessimism about the future of Amite County.

Pessimistic because Amite is such a desperately poor place to begin with. Pessimistic because so many of the young Negroes leave, and the bright and rebellious handful that stays is likely to be recruited into the Government's million-dollar anti-poverty Headstart program or else die in Vietnam. Throughout the state the potential second generation of the movement is being absorbed by such programs and the draft. Pessimistic because SNCC probably left Mississippi a year too soon, and the MFDP has expended too much of its energy in Washington, and not enough in remote outposts like Amite.

Nevertheless, three young Dantes, all under thirty years of age, have helped bring substantial change since July of 1961. The right to hold meetings and the right of civil-rights workers to move freely around the county have been won. The pattern of fear and submissiveness in the Negro community has been broken. Local leadership is developing. About 500 Negroes are registered, and at least 1,000 will be on the voting rolls by the time of the next countywide election in 1967. Such voting strength is, at least, enough to dilute the arbitrary terror.

Still, no Negro's life has been materially improved. Nor is there any visible possibility of such improvement. Amite remains the bottom of the iceberg, which only massive outside intervention, backed by the Federal Government, can shatter.

On my last night in Amite an old Negro preacher asked me what could possibly change the "conditions of my people?"

The only answer I could give him was the absurd fantasy that one day Lyndon Johnson, traveling in disguise as did Peter the Great, might come to Amite, and live for a few days on Steptoe's farm.

Chapter 5
SNCC

I have seen the best minds of my generation destroyed by madness.
—ALLEN GINSBERG

I weep because for my very life I cannot spin gold from straw.
—RUMPELSTILTSKIN

■ Inside that hermetic, vague community called the New Left, one word, above all others, has the magic to inspire blind loyalty and epic myth. SNCC.

But like a Picasso, or a Bob Dylan, or a Malcolm X, SNCC keeps reexamining its assumptions, changing its ideas, racing through periods faster than printers can set sober analyses into cold type. Abstract theories about this volatile and kaleidoscopic movement quickly become as dated as last season's batting averages. Howard Zinn's evocative book, *SNCC*, The New Abolitionists finished early in 1964, did not describe the SNCC that emerged from the Summer Project and convention challenge of that year. The perceptive report on the New Radicals by Paul Jacobs and Saul Landau published in the spring of 1966 has apparently been rendered obsolete by the dramatic SNCC staff retreat held at a campsite near Nashville from the 8th to the 15th of May, 1966. Even as the Jacobs-Landau volume was being rushed to bookstores, SNCC was choosing a new leader, a new strategy and a new set of assumptions.

There have been at least four separate SNCCs since its founding in 1960, and even these categories are outsiders' generalizations that ignore eddies and countertendencies that have always strained for expression just below the surface of this chaotic and decentralized organization.

SNCC began as a religious band of middle-class, rather square reformers, seeking only "our rights." The lunch counter was their entrance point to the revered American Dream of More. Their guiding spirit was not even Gandhi so much as the Bill of Rights, the 13th, 14th, and 15th Amendments, and the Holy Bible. They were black, liberal integrationists grappling with segregation.

By 1962 and 1963 SNCC workers had moved into the rural communities of the South. There they were shot, beaten, gassed, whipped, and jailed. They became a hardened nonviolent guerrilla army, challenging not merely segregation, but "the System," with voter registration, protest marches, and community organization. They learned that Northern corporations owned the racist mills in Danville, Virginia, and the segregating factories in Birmingham. But they still believed that America, if shamed with enough redemptive suffering, would honor its century-old pledge of equality for the black man.

The third SNCC emerged after the traumatic summer of 1964 in the image of Camus's existential rebel. The early innocent faith that the Federal Government would be the decisive force in ending segregation was shattered at the Democratic convention and by the fact that the killers of Goodman, Chaney, and Schwerner were never tried. This SNCC was in the clenched-fist tradition of the Russian Narodniks of the 1880's, and the American Populists of the same period. It believed in an alliance of the black and white underclass. It had a mystical and transcendental faith in the inherent goodness of the poor, and even in their infinite wisdom. It organized in the cities on "a priority of psychological damage": winos, junkies, hustlers, pimps, prostitutes; a concept rooted more in Genet's existential notion of an underclass than in the economic ones of Marx or Myrdal. The keynote words and phrases of this SNCC were *freedom, community, decentralization, local leadership, participatory democracy.*

Then, slowly, during 1965 and 1966, a new SNCC began to take shape inside the shell of the old existential SNCC. And this new nationalistic, revolutionary, independent SNCC, nurtured by pessimism and a hunger for manhood, was born in May, 1966, in Nashville, with the ouster of its gentle, religious chairman, John Lewis, and the ascension of brilliant, glib, complex, twenty-five-year-old Stokely Carmichael. Now the keynote phrases in SNCC are *independent black power, race pride, black dignity,* and *the third world,* a psychic crutch for a dead-end theory.

The twenty-five whites on the SNCC staff will now organize only poor whites. They will be kept out of the black community. Countywide, independent, all-black political parties will be organized, patterned after the Black Panther party, fashioned by Carmichael in Lowndes County. Implicitly, SNCC has given up on the over-thirty generation of fearful, church-loving Southern Negroes. They will now concentrate on organizing the new generation of Negroes, especially those on Southern campuses and in the riot-pocked cities of the North. SNCC will begin to try to fill the void left by the assassination of Malcolm X.

It is still much too early to try to evaluate SNCC's new direction. Nationalism may have its roots in wounded, destructive hatred, or in an ugly but necessary psycho-political strategy. Which thread is dominant in SNCC is unclear. Equally, it is too soon to tell whether SNCC sees its separatism as a temporary tactic to gain for the Negro psychic and political parity, or whether it is the eternal separation envisaged by the Black Muslims.

My intuition—and I pray that I am wrong—is that SNCC will never get the chance to play out its experiments fully. Already it has been described as "racist" by Roy Wilkins and it has been scolded by friends like Martin Luther King, the *New York Post* and *The New Republic.* Funds are beginning to dry up. The mass media are confusing nationalism with racism and self-defense with violence. I suspect that SNCC's new strategy is the doomed and gallant gesture of a captain going down with a sinking ship, standing at ramrod attention and saluting the flag.

The arguments against separatism are almost too obvious to make. Negroes are just 10 percent of a pluralistic society; they are a majority in no state, in no Southern congressional district. The Southern Negro is basically conservative and religious. Nationalism—however inevitable—will drive away the protective cover of liberal concern that has shielded SNCC at least a little, for the last six years. And nationalism can easily spill over into racism, as it has with LeRoi Jones. A white SNCC worker recently told me, "The Movement is really a search for the moral equivalent of blackness." There is a lot of this "White Negro" mythology in the New Left, and the deluded victims of this myth need constantly to be reminded of the immoral blackness of Tshombe, Duvalier, and Congressman Dawson. There is no inherent virtue in being black.

But even after all this is said, one then sympathizes with the hopeless but proud impulse that is the fuel for SNCC's nationalism. One needs only to recall a few of the betrayals of the American Dream that SNCC has suffered these last two years to comprehend that when all hope vanishes, a revolutionary pride still endures. As Mendy Samstein, a white SNCC veteran told me: "I curse this country every day of my life because it made me hate it, and I never wanted to." Mendy—and SNCC—hoped to weave the gold of Utopia from the straw of mid-century America.

In June of 1964 Mississippi Summer Project volunteers Andrew Goodman, James Chaney and Michael Schwerner were lynched and murdered and their killers are still free, respected members of their communities. In August of 1964 SNCC made what turned out to be its final request for entrance to the American Dream at the Democratic convention, where an integrated delegation sought to be seated in place of the regular, segregationist delegation from Mississippi.

Then Malcolm X, the shining black prince of ghetto youth was assassinated. The war in Vietnam continued to escalate and Santo Domingo was invaded by 20,000 marines because a popular revolution had 53 communists in its ranks. The anti-poverty Headstart program in Mississippi was emasculated by Sargent Shriver, under pressure from Senators Stennis and Eastland. SNCC communications director Julian Bond was twice elected to the Georgia state legislature from Atlanta's 136th district—and twice he was denied his seat because he opposed the war in Vietnam. Mississippi Negroes, homeless and hungry, set up a tent city across the street from the White House to dramatize their plight, but President Johnson refused even to see them. Terror by whites against blacks continued in the deep South; in the "model city" of Tuskeegee, Samual Younge, a college student active with SNCC was killed. The Mississippi legislature gerrymandered out of existence the 2nd delta district, because it had a Negro population majority. In the Alabama Democratic primary, white integrationist Richmond Flowers was swamped, local Negro candidates defeated, and Mrs. George Wallace elected Governor. Near Hernando, Mississippi, this June, 15 FBI agents could do nothing as a sniper in ambush pumped 50 shotgun pellets into James Meredith.

The Dream deferred, "dried up, like a raisin in the sun."

Two other factors contributed to the creation of the new SNCC in Nashville. One was the general decline of the civil-rights movement as a national force after the Selma demonstrations of February and March of 1965. Since then, the passage of the Voting Rights Bill lulled liberals into the illusion that The Problem had been solved, and the riots in Watts turned moderate feeling in the country sharply against civil rights. Further, the war in Vietnam and ghetto poverty began to absorb the energies of student activists. And almost all the strategies for change in the South seemed implausible. The civil-rights movement had reached an impasse, with aimless frustrations building up fury behind the barrier of insoluble problems.

Meanwhile, SNCC itself began to deteriorate internally. The number of organizers in the field fell from 200 in late 1964 to 120 in the winter of 1966. The prophetic band that had provided the rest of the freedom movement with so many new ideas, grew stale, repeating old formulas. Programs like all-out support of the MFDP congressional challenge and attempts at urban organizing in Montgomery, Birmingham, and Atlanta proved to be failures. Factionalism increased inside SNCC, and large numbers gathered around Bob Parris and began to drift off into other directions, some to organize on their own, others to form a bohemian sub-culture in New York's East Village. Drinking, auto accidents, petty thievery, pot smoking, personality clashes, inefficiency, and anti-white outbursts all increased inside SNCC during this period. The mood of SNCC on the eve of the Nashville staff retreat was sullen and desperate for life.

The minutes of the Nashville meeting read like a group therapy session, or more likely, a macabre sequel to Genet's *The Blacks*.

For a whole week the staff met, over 130 people, including 25 whites. All had been jailed, all had known hunger and exhaustion, most, including the 20 girls, had been beaten. James Forman, who was stepping down as executive secretary, had a bleeding ulcer and a heart ailment. Ivanhoe Donaldson had his scalp shattered in Danville, Virginia. John Lewis suffered a fractured skull in Selma. Gloria Larry had seen Reverend Jonathan Daniels murdered on the streets of Haynesville, Alabama.

There were open expressions of anti-white feeling at the meeting. White staffers were sometimes taunted and mocked when they tried to speak. One field secretary seriously suggested SNCC ar-rarange for 100 Negroes to study nuclear physics at UCLA and then be sent to an African country to help it construct an atomic bomb to "blow up America." Another proposed that only the black press and the African press be invited to all future SNCC press conferences.

But the dominant figures in the emerging SNCC—Carmichael, Courtland Cox, Charley Cobb and Ivanhoe Donaldson—spoke *not in racist terms—but in nationalist terms,* insisting on the necessity *of independent black political, economic, and cultural institutions.* They said whites could no longer organize blacks. They said, "Being pro-black was not being anti-white." Carmichael at one point exclaimed, "Man, I'm not in that racist bag—I just dig black."

Early in the meeting Carmichael ran against Lewis for chairman, backed primarily by his fellow organizers of the Black Panther party. Lewis was reelected 60 to 22.

Then the staffers began a grotesquely honest exploration of the assumptions of their organization. Gradually the realization grew that they no longer believed integration into the American Dream was possible or desirable, and that any contact with white mainstream institutions was damaging to black psyches. It was at this point that the election of Lewis, a popular but not authoritative symbol of SNCC's religious and moral past, was reopened.

Lewis told his former cellmates that he wanted to attend the upcoming White House Conference on Civil Rights. The staff voted to boycott the conference. Lewis insisted he had joined in the planning sessions and would go in defiance of the staff decision. On the second vote Carmichael was chosen the new chairman of SNCC by a vote of 60 to 12. The SNCC of Camus and James Baldwin and Fannie Lou Hamer was suddenly a nostalgic chapter of radical history. And a new SNCC was forged in the stark image of Malcolm X, Frantz Fanon, and John Brown. America had its first indigenous revolutionary movement since the Wobblies.

With intentional symbolism, the first act of the new SNCC was the release of its statement rejecting the invitation to the White House Conference on Civil Rights. Couched in the exaggerated cadences of an underground manifesto, the statement read:

The student Nonviolent Coordinating Committee believes the White House conference entitled To Secure These

Rights is absolutely unnecessary and rejects its invitation to participate in this useless endeavor for the following reasons:

1. The foundation and consequences of racism are not rooted in the behavior of black Americans, yesterday or today. They are rooted in an attempt by Europeans and white Americans to exploit and dehumanize the descendants of Africa for monetary gain. This process of universal exploitation of Africa and her descendants continues today by the power elite of this country. In the process of exploiting black Americans, white America has tried to shift the responsibility for the degrading position in which blacks now find themselves away from the oppressors to the oppressed. The White House conference, especially with its original focus on the Negro family as the main problem with which America must deal, accentuates this process of shifting the burden of the problem.

2. Regardless of the proposals which stem from this conference, we know that the executive department and the President are not serious about insuring Constitutional rights to black Americans. For example, murderers of civil rights workers and black citizens roam free in this country with the desire to kill more freedom fighters; and the national government claims it is impotent in many situations to bring about justice. For example, police chiefs, sheriffs and state officials who have victimized black people, beaten and jailed them and further suppressed our dignity are fully aware they were in effect given a blank check by the executive department of the government to inflict these lawless acts upon Negroes, since it is common knowledge throughout the South that killing a "nigger" is like killing a coon.

3. We believe that the President has called this conference within the U.S. at a time when U.S. prestige internationally is at a low ebb due to our involvement in the Vietnam civil war, the Dominican Republic, the Congo, South Africa and other parts of the Third World.

We cannot be a party to attempts by the White House to use black Americans to recoup prestige lost internationally.

4. Our organization is opposed to the war in Vietnam and we cannot in good conscience meet with the chief policy maker of the Vietnam war to discuss human rights in this country when he flagrantly violates the human rights of colored people in Vietnam.

5. We reaffirm our belief that people who suffer must make the decisions about how to change and direct their lives. We therefore call upon all black Americans to begin building independent political, economic, and cultural institutions that they will control and use as instruments of social change in this country.

The next day Carmichael, lounging in the Atlanta SNCC office in T-shirt and faded dungarees, told the press that the Black Panther party would not seek Federal protection or observers in the Alabama election on November 8th. The party's all-Negro countywide slate of candidates, he said, would be "protected by the toughest Negroes we can find in Watts, Harlem, Chicago, and Washington. . . . We have discovered the Justice Department cats just take notes and never do anything to protect our people, or to stop voting frauds by whites."

The first time I met Stokely Carmichael was in August of 1961. I was a reporter for a weekly newspaper in the Bronx and he, a Bronx resident, had just come out of the infamous Parchmann State Reformatory in Mississippi, after serving forty-nine days as a freedom rider. During the interview he said, "You know how dumb them crackers are? In jail they took away all my books— stuff by Du Bois, King, Camus. But they let me keep Mills' book about Castro, *Listen, Yankee*, because they thought it was against Northern agitators."

The next time I met Stokely was in Lowndes County in the spring of 1965. He had been there three months and there already had been one murder. Fear paralyzed the energy of the black community, which outnumbered whites 4 to 1. Stokely broke that fear by taunting the sheriff, walking behind him in broad daylight, mocking his stride, mimicking his dress, and cursing him in Yiddish: "Kish mir tuchas, baby," he said.

The next time I saw him was four months later at a press conference in the New York SNCC office, which he held on the way back from Reverend Jonathan Daniels' funeral in Keene, New Hampshire.

The four months in Lowndes had changed him more than the four years between our first two meetings. The manic emotionalism was gone, replaced by the somber serenity of a man, now twenty-five, resigned to early death. The lean, tall athletic body was beginning to develop the "starch fat" of the poor; Stokely's angular face was becoming puffy from his diet of greens and spices. He was no longer a wisecracking performer. He was a revolutionary who said, "Look, man, I've been to seventeen funerals since 1961. I know I'm going to die, but that just makes me work all the harder and faster, dig?"

Stokely was brought by his parents from Trinidad to the Negro ghetto in the Bronx in 1952, when he was eleven years old. Just as Bob Parris—a hero to Stokely—broke out of Harlem by attending Stuyvesant High School, Stokely overcame his environment and passed the rigorous entrance examination for the Bronx High School of Science.

Carmichael lived a double life; winning good grades and going to posh parties downtown with his white friends, and running with a wild gang in Harlem, fighting, stealing, smoking pot. His teachers at Bronx High told him he would become "a brilliant Negro leader"; his Negro friends in Harlem called him a faggot for reading books. And Stokely reflected upon the famous quote of W.E.B. Du Bois:

One ever feels his two-ness—an American, a Negro—two souls, two thoughts, two unreconciled strivings; two warring ideals in one dark body, whose dogged strength alone keeps it from being torn asunder. The history of the American Negro is the history of this strife . . . this longing to attain self-conscious manhood, to merge his double self into a better and truer self.

Stokely resolved his "two-ness" by going to almost-all-Negro Howard University in September of 1960 and majoring, like Parris and Mario Savio, in philosophy.

But all through Howard, where he was a classmate of Courtland Cox, Charley Cobb, and a dozen other future SNCC field secretaries, there were pilgrimages to the South. Slowly, his colorful, cocky, creative personality made him one of SNCC's leaders among equals. When the 1964 Summer Project came, Stokely was made director for the 2nd Congressional District in the delta.

As writers and journalists poured over that wounded land that summer, legends and tales of Stokely began to filter into the national press. That he was SNCC's wildest driver quickly became part of the myth. In *The New Abolitionists*, Howard Zinn wrote that Stokely "would stride, cool and smiling through Hell, philosophizing all the way." By the end of the summer, there was a 100-member national organization with the initials FASC—standing for the Friends and Admirers of Stokely Carmichael. And every few days there arrived in the SNCC office in Jackson a package for Stokely from some local chapter of the FASC, filled with insect repellent, delicacies, shaving cream, cigarettes, and magazines. After some bragging and strutting, he would always share his bounty with the less visible SNCC organizers.

In January of 1965 Stokely, along with Courtland Cox and Bob Mantz, moved into Lowndes County, Alabama, where not one of the 12,000 Negroes was registered, and white registration was 117 percent. Later Stokely was to say of his venture into Alabama's most feared county, "I just got into that Bob Moses [Parris] bag. I had to see what I could do in the place no one else would go."

On March 25, 1965, Mrs. Viola Gregg Liuzzo was killed in

Lowndes as she ferried civil-rights workers between Montgomery and Selma at the finish of the protest march of 50,000 led by Martin Luther King that day.

In August, Reverend Jonathan Daniels was shot dead in Hayneville, the sleepy county seat of Lowndes, and Father Richard Morrisroe was seriously wounded. Three SNCC field secretaries—Willie Vaughn, Ruby Sales and Gloria Larry, plus a local girl, Joyce Bailey, saw Thomas Coleman, a fifty-two-year-old shopkeeper and part-time deputy sheriff, shoot the two clergymen. Two trials failed to convict Coleman.

In the fall there was a school boycott and then participation in the Agricultural Stabilization and Conservation Service (ASCS) election, which elects a local board that determines crucial allotments for cotton acreage and subsidies. There were massive frauds and the Negro candidates lost, although they constituted a 4 to 1 majority among the farmers eligible to vote.

Meanwhile, with the passage of the 1965 Voting Rights Act, the Justice Department appointed a Federal registrar for Lowndes County. Lashed by the sharp-tongued goads and organizing skills of the SNCC workers, Lowndes Negroes began to register. When Stokely arrived in January, not one Negro was on the voting rolls; eleven months later, Negro registration passed 2,000, matching that of the overregistered whites in the county.

In November, the SNCC organizers decided to form a separate political party at the county unit level in Lowndes and in six nearby counties. At a meeting of about 100 liberal and radical intellectuals held in Washington that month, following the SANE-sponsored march against the Vietnam war, Carmichael, a hypnotic orator, said:

> The county courthouse has always been the symbol of oppression for the rural Negro. But we are going to make it the symbol of liberation. . . . We're going to emancipate the Black Belt courthouse by courthouse, starting with Lowndes. We're gonna build political parties run by poor people that

will run candidates for everything that runs. We're going to elect sheriffs, school boards, tax assessors, everything in Lowndes County with our party. We're gonna call it the Black Panther.

The liberals cheered and promised money.

Stokely went back into the community and began to organize for the nominating convention in May and the statewide ballot in November. There were emotional mass meetings and the democratic nomination of candidates. Stokely wanted an all-black ticket, but the more conservative local Negroes wanted an integrated ticket. Stokely asked a local Negro, "You're all black, ain't you, so what's wrong with an all-black slate?"

But in true SNCC style, Stokely agreed to "let the people decide." When no local whites would run under the symbol of the charging black panther, he felt vindicated.

On May 3rd, on the steps of the same courthouse in Hayneville where Tom Coleman was acquitted for the murder of Reverend Daniels, 900 Negroes assembled to formally nominate their slate of candidates. Almost all of them had guns. Lowndes had become what the Pike-Amite project was to SNCC in 1961—the only place where it could claw a beachhead. So it was understandable that two weeks later the floundering movement should turn to Stokely to put it back on the path that had bathed it with the aura of myth only two years before.

The unions, the liberals, the moderate civil-rights leaders, have all displayed their displeasure at SNCC's nationalist direction, expressions equally as logical and inevitable as SNCC's policy. As Carmichael once put it, "Man, every cat's politics comes from what he sees when he gets up in the morning. The liberals see Central Park and we see sharecropper shacks."

Even before the Nashville meeting, SNCC's historic contributions to the freedom movement tended to be down-graded by the "Negro expert" industry spawned by the movement. Few of the instant historians would admit—or possibly knew—that it was SNCC who first ventured into the wasteland of Mississippi, who first organized Selma, two years before the big march, who first conceived the watershed of the 1964 Mississippi Summer Project.

The arrogant victims of SNCC are now in for a long season in hell. The Klan, HUAC, the unions, the moderates, the press, the Uncle Toms, they will all hound—and isolate—SNCC, and then try to peck out its vitals like a modern Prometheus. In a half century detached scholars—who will have the admitted benefit of no contact with the race-haunted kamikazes of SNCC—will probably enshrine its organizers alongside those other singing Utopians, Wobblies. In fifty years Stokely may be mythicized like Joe Hill is today, but SNCC now will be treated the way the IWW was in 1917.

The root of the SNCC tragedy is, I suppose, the larger fate of the whole Southern freedom movement, which now seems at a dead end, invigorated only by occasional outrages like the shooting of James Meredith. Every symptom is that the Southern movement is now burnt out, exhausted by unredemptive suffering, cynical because daily conditions are so little changed in fundamental ways.

It is a joyless desperation that fuels SNCC's gamble with black nationalism today. It is the final, heroic gesture of proud Cyrano, jabbing his glistening blade at fate.

Perhaps these desperate pioneers, who created the sit-ins, the freedom rides, the freedom parties, the summer projects, the whole superstructure of myth that illuminated the freedom movement for one historical moment, perhaps they now believe that only their own final destruction can somehow prove to the nonwhite majority on this planet the utter wretchedness of the nation they tried so long to reform and redeem.

Chapter 6
SDS

We seek the establishment of a democracy of individual participation governed by two central aims: That the individual share in those social decisions determining the quality and direction of his life; that society be organized to encourage independence in men and provide the media for their common participation.
—FOUNDING MANIFESTO OF STUDENTS FOR A
DEMOCRATIC SOCIETY

Build not burn—SDS SLOGAN

■ *As the United Airline's jetliner circled over gray Chicago and* glistening Lake Michigan, I felt like a pilgrim coming home. Each feeling and thought was magnified and self-consciously examined. But I was returning home not to a city, but to a generation, a movement, and an organization.

In 1962 I had been a full-time activist in Students for a Democratic Society in the months prior to its founding convention at Port Huron, Michigan, and immediately after it, when the organization scratched and clawed to survive in the jungle of "youth politics."

I had written crisis leaflets, endured endless meetings, shared the communion of the picket line and the "pride" of a civil-rights arrest in Maryland. Now I was coming to Chicago to interview the new generation of SDS leaders and evaluate their organization and ideas, not as picket-line partisan but as journalist.

In 1962 SDS had consisted of about 200 committed activists and 10 functioning campus chapters. It had meager resources and seemed stuck together with staples and dreams. Mailings rarely went out on time from the cramped office on East 19th Street in Manhattan. Many of the nominal members owed primary loyalty to other organizations, and saw SDS as an arena from which to recruit. SDS was then just one of a dozen radical student groups, setting sail under the first winds of change on the campuses. It was smaller than the Student Peace Union, CORE, campus Americans for Democratic Action, and the Young People's Socialist League; about the same size as New University Thought and the Northern Student Movement; larger only than the Marxist sects.

But by October of 1965, when I made my pilgrimage to Chicago, SDS had become the largest and most respected of all the campus-based groups on the New Left. The single-issue SPU had disintegrated after the test-ban treaty was signed. CORE fell apart as SNCC became the spearhead of the Southern freedom movement. NUT was never an activist group and disappeared during 1963. YPSL fell into the hands of neo-Trotskyites and was disowned by its parent Socialist Party. Campus ADA was filled with tweedy careerists and shunned by the new militants. Only SDS, with its activist program, multi-issue, nonideological approach, and seriousness, had grown steadily since 1962.

SDS members like Steve Weissman and Eric Levine were at the heart of the Berkeley FSM. Future SDS presidents Tom Hayden and Paul Potter were beaten in McComb, Mississippi, in October of 1961, long before it became fashionable to penetrate the Closed Society. SDS ground out a steady flow of pamphlets and documents, all of exceptional intellectual caliber. SDS organized a march of 20,000 on Washington to protest the war in Vietnam. The teach-in movement was born in Ann Arbor, with the help of the biggest chapter of SDS. SDS was the first Northern student group to begin community organization of the ghettoes, in the style of SNCC. Through a complex network of personal friendships, SDS became SNCC's closest ally and fiercest defender. And SDS, in the autumn of 1965, began organizing directly against the draft, and was attacked for it by the Justice Department, the FBI, the Senate, and much of the national press.

Upon my arrival in Chicago I found the organization as I had left it—in the maelstrom of crisis. It was under nationally head-lined assault from Attorney General Katzenbach and respected senators like Mansfield and Kuchel, as well as from right-wing spokesmen like Dodd, Thurmond, and Stennis. It was in the midst of splitting "amicably" from its parent organization, the League for Industrial Democracy. It had just resolved a factional dispute between the hipsters and the intellectuals in favor of the latter. It was busy preparing a response to a snide attack printed a few weeks before by *The New Leader*. And it was gaining new members at a rate many of its leaders considered organizationally dangerous.

The SDS national headquarters is located between two empty storefronts under the East 63rd Street el in the heavily Negro Woodlawn section of Chicago. It shares a debris-littered street with a beauty parlor, a check-cashing service, a fried chicken joint, and a record shop that continuously blares the soulful blues of Ray Charles.

The organization had moved to Chicago from New York five months before, to be centrally located geographically and to escape the atmosphere of the "Old Left tribes" that prevailed in New York.

The SDS national office consists of ten chaotic, poorly lighted rooms, filled with clacking typewriters, ringing telephones, and boisterous activists. The walls are freckled with symbols of almost every political faction. There is a poster Picasso designed for the Italian Communist Party; there is a charcoal drawing of Eugene Debs; several IWW stickers; an MFDP poster; a print by Ben Shahn; a Feiffer cartoon; newspaper photographs of Bob Dylan; and the slogan, "Make love, not war."

The symptoms of office living abound—an unmade cot, several

laundry bags, a jar of instant coffee, and a half-eaten chocolate bar. There are books by Ken Kesey and Norman O. Brown.

And, inevitably, on the wall is a model mimeograph machine, and beneath it, the hand-drawn motto: "Our Founder."

The almost all-white, all middle-class membership of SDS is estimated, as of April 1, 1966, at 5,500, distributed in 151 chapters in thirty-seven states. But given SDS's reticence about aggressive recruiting, its sloppy accounting, and the New Radical's nonjoining instinct, these figures probably do not reveal the group's true strength on the campuses. National secretary Paul Booth, a witty twenty-two-year-old graduate of Swarthmore, estimates that for every member, five others take part in SDS activity without paying dues.

The membership is diverse, encompassing high-school students, college students, college dropouts, hipsters, beatniks, teaching assistants, and about 300 faculty members. There are liberals, rebels, and revolutionaries; community organizers and university scholars; potheads and Puritans; the sons and daughters of Republicans and Communists, of professors and plumbers.

Generally, the membership can be broken down into five broad categories. One consists of those members on small rural campuses in the Midwest and Far West who are only vaguely liberal, politically unsophisticated, and unable to tell a Spartacist from a narcissist. These members are more interested in combating the Radical Right or in protesting against campus curfews than in burning draft cards or debating whether Bayard Rustin has sold out. They are, in fact, rather frightened by talk of socialism and by the bizarre stunts pulled by some of the apocalyptic militants in SDS. They are idealistic types unable to find any adequate receptacle for that idealism anywhere in the Great Society. They don't find it in their football- and fraternity-crazed universities, or in their families, or in their churches. The instincts of these SDSers in Kansas, North Dakota, and Oklahoma are authentically patriotic, but then they see civil-rights cases ruled on by segregationist judges, wars on poverty generaled by hack politicians, and an undemocratic government in Saigon defended by napalm. They are taught the Bill of Rights in History One, but then they see the Attorney General smear and investigate their own organization because it exercises the freedoms guaranteed by the Bill of Rights. They are taught that America stands for justice and law and order, yet they know that Andy Goodman's murderer is still a sheriff in Mississippi. These patriotic Populists are the newest dimension to SDS, following the political intellectuals and the alienated hippies into the SDS melting pot. Their influence will probably be particularly beneficial as hysteria over the Vietnam war and a possible return of McCarthyism exacerbates the organization's kamikaze wing. They will be a ballast of moderation.

The second influential grouping in SDS is the Old Guard, those students who founded and built up the organization in 1962, and who are now in their middle twenties and are either finishing graduate school or teaching in college. This grouping includes Dick Flacks, now an instructor at the University of Chicago; Bob Ross, former SDS vice president, now doing graduate work in sociology at the University of Chicago; national staff members Paul Booth and Todd Gitlin; and former president Al Haber. Members of this group are all earnest political intellectuals, with impressive tools of scholarship and analysis.

The third large chunk of the SDS membership falls into the apolitical hipster-anarchist camp. Many in this group joined SDS in response to the war in Vietnam. They wear long hair, smoke pot, dig Dylan and rock 'n' roll, and like to hobo around the country from project to project. They are skeptical of all centralized authority, predetermined programs, and formal voting, and even tried to abolish the posts of national secretary and president in favor of rotation and Quaker consensus.

These spiritual, if not philosophical, anarchists, however, have also been a positive influence on SDS. They help keep the organization's focus on the grass roots and have taught it the cheapness of five-vote majorities. They help contribute to the climate of individual respect and tolerance that permeates SDS, whereby no one is ever shouted down or ruled out of order at meetings, no matter how irrelevant his speech may be. Anarchism has always been more effective as a personal ethical code than as a strategy for social change, and as such, its contribution to SDS's pluralism should not be undervalued. Many of the newer recruits to SDS say they joined simply because of the warmth and integrity of the older members. As a freshman from Piedmont College put it, "I just decided these are the best human beings around, and figured it is with them I should make the good fight. That way, even if you lose, you gain something very valuable."

The fourth SDS grouping is composed of the approximately 75 full-time organizers working on the ghetto projects. This group exists independently of the rest of SDS in the Economic Research and Action Project (ERAP), and its members closely resemble SNCC workers in their outlook and life style. They are very patient about social change; they speak with an almost religious love of the poor with whom they work; and some of them are just as alienated and scarred as a SNCC worker from the delta. They have seen slum parents sit up all night with a baseball bat, guarding their child's crib against rats. They have seen welfare checks handed over to junk pushers. They have seen ten-year-old girls who have learned to fight like boys twice their age. Like the SNCC worker, they see and judge all of America with the bitter eye of the victim.

The last—and largest—are the hundreds of ordinary career-orientated, liberal intellectuals on the major eastern campuses.

There is an appalling anti-intellectualism among the newer SDS members. Not only do they read few novels and almost no scientific or philosophical literature, they have read little within the radical tradition. Of twenty-five activists interviewed, none had ever read Rosa Luxemburg, Max Weber, Eduard Bernstein, John Dewey, Peter Kropotkin, or John Stuart Mill. Less than five had actually read Lenin or Trotsky, and only a few more had ever read Marx. Almost all of them had read C. Wright Mills and Camus, and about half had read Goodman, Frantz Fanon, and Herbert Marcuse. More had read *The Realist* than had read Mill's "Essay on Liberty," or the "Sermon on the Mount." When asked what the last novel they had read was, seven couldn't remember. Other answers included the autobiographical *Manchild in the Promised Land; Sometimes a Great Notion; Candy; V; Drive, He Said; Last Exit to Brooklyn;* and *Making Do.* All the novels had been published within the last two years, and most dealt with the decadence or absurdity of life.

Most of those questioned justified their sparse reading by saying either that they had little to learn from the past or that the demands of activism took up most of their time. Even the few who regretted never having read Mill and Weber insisted they could learn more from events that touched their own lives than from any book.

The notion of "nonleadership" and the fear of manipulation are definitive characteristics of the New Left. So it is that in SDS there is no *one leader*, not even a cadre of eight or ten who make basic policy decisions. Instead, power is shared by the National Council of about 35 members and the "Chicago kernel" of about 15 who work out of the national office. Except for the gap between the sophisticated and the naïve, all the other disparities within the organization are reflected inside the leadership, from ideological and Puritanical Steve Max in New York, to anarchic and sensitive Jeff Shero in Texas, to Carl Oglesby, the playwright and ex-actor who is now SDS's president.

The following are sketches of three of the more influential of SDS's nonleaders.

The individual who has imprinted his Protean personality most strongly on SDS is twenty-six-year-old Tom Hayden, the organization's first president, primary drafter of the *Port Huron Statement*, and architect of the strategy of community organization of the ghettoes.

I first met Hayden early in 1962, shortly after he had celebrated his twenty-second birthday in a cold jail cell in Albany, Georgia. Already his writing had been published by *Liberation* and *Dissent,* and he had written a pamphlet called *Revolution in Mississippi.* He was then a moderate radical, strongly influenced by Michael Harrington and Albert Camus. He had many friends active in SNCC.

But over the years Hayden's politics have grown increasingly more revolutionary and bitter, and he has lost his faith in cooperation with liberals and moderate socialists like his one-time influence, Harrington. The writings of Mills, Marx, and Weber, and wrenching experiences in the South, deepened Hayden's radicalism, and organizational in-fighting with adult leaders in the civil-rights movement and in the LID alienated him from the more bureaucratic, more anti-Communist Old Left.

Hayden is now an organizer for the Newark Community Union Project (NCUP) and a contributing editor to both *Liberation* and *Studies on the Left.* An idol to many of the new recruits to SDS, he now tries to keep away from national SDS meetings, fleeing from his leadership role, retreating deeper into the squalid slums of Newark.

My own intuition is that Hayden's Catholic upbringing helps explain at least part of his absolutist radicalism. He has an overwhelming sense of the sinfulness of the affluent, "quasi-fascist" society; for him, to organize the outcasts of Newark is the equivalent of a religious fast—penance for the sins of status committed in Sodom.

Few in the New Left combine Hayden's innovative intellect, sensitivity to experience, and writing craftsmanship. If he ever pauses in his fast to redeem Sodom, he may someday write an American version of Fanon's *The Wretched of the Earth.*

Bearded, slouched, thirty-year-old father of three, Carl Oglesby is the current president of SDS. Less political and more romantic than Hayden, he is close to being the archetypal New Leftist.

Oglesby, who looks a little like D. H. Lawrence, was born in

1935 in Akron, Ohio, of working-class and later divorced parents. He attended Kent State University, dropped out to spend a year in Greenwich Village, and then returned to earn his degree. As with Parris and Forman of SNCC, there followed a period of intellectual searching through the desert of the 1950's, as if waiting for a social movement to rescue him from his ennui.

Oglesby began to write plays. One was produced by a theatre group in Dallas, and another read at the Actors Studio in New York. Two others, *The Hero* and *The Peacemaker*, were produced at the University of Michigan. There is also an unfinished novel in Oglesby's past.

In June of 1965 Oglesby was making twelve thousand dollars a year with the Bendix Systems Division at Ann Arbor; "a hireling in the Cold War," he has said of himself. Then at the SDS convention he was nominated for president and elected over four rivals. In a classic Narodnik gesture, he quit his affluent job in the corporate hierarchy to become the face and voice of SDS for a token salary that often went unpaid.

"There is something very Emersonian about SDS," Oglesby has told several interviewers, and that is true. The comment also reflects the romantic, transcendence-seeking core of Oglesby's own radicalism, which is admittedly nonprogrammatic. This quality was sharply reflected in the Shakespearean-cadenced speech Oglesby delivered to the annual dinner of the *National Guardian* in November of 1965. He said in part:

At our best, I think we (SDS) are SNCC translated to the North and trained on a somewhat different and broader set of issues. Our best concern comes from SNCC. Some find that concern a bit shocking, but I'll name it anyway. It is to make love more possible. We work to remove from society what threatens and prevents it—the inequity that coordinates with injustice to create plain suffering and to make custom of distrust. Poverty. Racism. The assembly line universities of this Pepsi Generation. The ulcerating drive for affluence.

And the ideology of anti-communism, too, because it smothers my curiosity and bribes my compassion. This ideology decrees to me that I may not love Castro, however shining-bright his anguish. . . .

Paul Booth, SDS's boyish-looking, twenty-two-year-old national secretary, is cut from a different, more political, more pragmatic cloth.

As a freshman at Swarthmore, Booth was a delegate to the founding convention of SDS at Port Huron, in 1962. I remember him then as a liberal Democrat, writing papers analyzing Democratic Party politics and engaged in the internecine intrigues of NSA. He had worked actively in John Kennedy's 1960 campaign, and his parents were influential members of ADA.

Over the years Booth's politics have grown more grass-roots oriented and more hostile to the national organs of liberalism, more in tune with the liberation movements of the Third World. But his politics have never lost their relatedness to the reality of political power. Booth can name most of the 435 congressmen; he follows closely the hearings by Senate subcommittees on relevant legislation; he knows what insurgents are planning Democratic Party primary fights six months in advance. He is of the world.

He was working as an organizer for the SDS community project in Oakland when, in the fall of 1965, he was drafted to bring "order and politics" to the SDS organization as the national secretary. Booth admits he is more "political" than most of SDS, but adds, "My job is to politicize the organization and give it some form, and to make sure there is real internal political education. . . . SDS has to be more than just an outlet for personal frustrations. It has to have a tangible effect on the society."

Hayden the revolutionary; Oglesby the romantic; Booth the realist; different, yet united by an intransigent, egalitarian radicalism that binds SDS together the way the melody gives unity to a free-form jazz improvisation.

SDS's pluralism, shared leadership, and aversion to hard ideology forces any discussion of its collective politics to be tentative and impressionistic. Its membership contains everything from ADA liberals to supporters of the Vietcong. But there seem to be several pillars of consensus upon which the pluralistic radicalism rests. They are the notions of participatory democracy; a moral idealism; and a refusal to participate in the Communist-anti-Communist debate.

The clearest exposition of participatory democracy came in the *Port Huron Statement,* which said:

In a participatory democracy, the political life would be based on several root principles:

That decision-making of basic social consequence be carried on by public groupings; that politics be seen positively, as the art of collectively creating an acceptable pattern of social relations; that politics has the function of bringing people out of isolation and into community, this being a necessary, but not sufficient, way of finding meaning in personal life; that the political order should serve to clarify problems in a way instrumental to their solution; it should provide outlets for the expression of personal grievance and aspiration; opposing views should be organized so as to illuminate choices and facilitate the attainment of goals; channels should be commonly available to relate men to knowledge and to power so that private problems from bad recreation facilities to personal alienation are formulated as general issues.

The economic sphere would have as its basis the principles: That work should involve incentives worthier than money or survival. It should be educative, not stultifying; creative, not mechanical; self-direct, not manipulated; encouraging independence, a respect for others, a sense of dignity and a willingness to accept social responsibility, since it is this experience that has crucial influence on habits, perceptions and individual ethics;

That the economic experience is so personally decisive that the individual must share in its full determination;

That the economy itself is of such social importance that its major resources and means of production should be open to democratic participation and subject to democratic social regulation.

The kernel of participatory democracy—the importance of the individual and his ability to make meaningful decisions that affect his life—led SDS to be critical of existing bureaucratic structures like the Democratic Party, unions, and the NAACP, and to go into the ghetto and organize the poor into their own organizations.

SDS, however, has tried to burden participatory democracy with the freight of both ideology and program, and that has been a mistake. Participatory democracy is a vague, Utopian ideal. It is also a therapeutic and effective organizing technique, but it is not the cornerstone for a theory of social change. It can be exciting, and even moving, to watch participatory democracy practiced in a slum project, as some unknown Northern equivalent of Fannie Lou Hamer overcomes fear and embarrassment to speak and think and finally energize those around her. But PD, as some aficionados call it, breaks down at conventions of four hundred students, or under the pressure of crisis decisions. And built into participatory democracy is no theory of the agent of social change that can create the society where ordinary individuals are permitted—and competent—to make basic decisions. SDS has thus far failed to examine critically the ramifications of participatory democracy. Are students *really* qualified to determine college curriculums? Can the poor *really* make technical decisions about the war on poverty? Do ordinary people *really* have enough information to make foreign-policy judgments? Can minority groups *really* control a civilian review board of the police without bias? These are complicated questions and should be dealt with thoughtfully, and not with a slogan, no matter how democratic and inspirational that slogan is.

A-historical and action-accented, the politics of SDS are rooted in ethical values. One activist called it the "post-Nuremberg ethic . . . which means every individual is totally morally responsible for everything he does."

When SDSers are posed with a possible strategy they ask themselves not, "Is it workable?" or "How much support can we get on this from the liberals?" They ask themselves, "Is it right to do this?" Most SDS members seem to be against the war in Vietnam not primarily because they think it is imperialistic or they fear a world war with China; they are against it because they feel they cannot participate in a war that demands they murder innocent peasants. Again, this is an invocation of the post-Nuremberg ethic —every man is responsible for his actions, including murder, and at some moment he must say no to the machine and the officers giving the orders to kill. The adjectives the SDSers invoke most frequently to condemn Johnson's Great Society are not "reactionary" or "militaristic," but "ethically corrupt" and "hypocritical."

Until recently the moral purity of SDS's dissent has worked against the formation of specific programs and theories about the makeup of the society. Another demonstration seemed to be the stock recipe for all intellectual problems, another chorus of a freedom song a substitute for analysis.

But in December of 1965 SDS held an educational conference at the University of Illinois that pointed the organization on a more reflective and analytical course. More than 400 members attended the workshops and debates. Slogans like "A change is gonna come" and "Let the people decide" began to be examined critically for the first time. It is still too early to measure the effects of the conference, but it indicated a healthy sense of curiosity and self-criticism inside SDS, portents of a more intellectually tough-minded future.

It is easy to misunderstand SDS's attitude toward Communism. Many liberals and trade unionists who fought the Stalinists in the 30's and 40's sincerely believe SDS is infiltrated by Communists, and its policies dangerously compromised on the questions of popular frontism and authoritarianism.

My own feeling, based on membership in SDS and friendship with several of its "leaders," is that SDS is non-Communist rather than anti-Communist; its leadership emotionally more antagonistic to red-baiters than reds, but without any real attraction to any of the varieties of Communist experience as a model for social change. SDS differs from its critics in organizations like the LID, ADA, and SANE in that it will not exclude *anyone* from membership, and it will not publicly engage in anti-Communist rhetoric. SDSers believe the savage struggles between Stalinists and Social Democrats contributed heavily to the failure of the Old Left, and they are determined not to repeat that chapter of history.

The Port Huron manifesto stated: "Many liberals and socialists share static and repetitious participation in the anti-Communist crusade and often discourage tentative inquiring discussion about the 'Russian question' within their ranks. . . . It would seem, too, that there should be a way for a person or an organization to oppose communism without contributing to the common fear of associations and public actions."

Later the manifesto goes on to conclude: "Communist parties throughout the world are generally undemocratic in internal structure and mode of action. Moreover, in most cases they subordinate radical programs to requirements of Soviet foreign policy. The communist movement has failed, in every sense, to achieve its stated intentions of leading a world-wide movement for human emancipation."

SDSers are often critical of the Communists and their sympathizers from the Left. An SDS Berkeley activist complains that

ILWU president Harry Bridges refuses to honor student picket lines protesting his union's shipment of arms to Vietnam. The same student asserted, "The communist kids were the most finky and cautious types in the FSM. They were all hung up about respectability and the mainstream, always looking to blunt the moral thrust of the movement, always looking to make a deal."

There *is* a problem, however, in SDS's attitude toward authoritarianism, but it doesn't derive from Communist financial backers, infiltration by Maoist agents, or leaders with "secret politics," as some have darkly hinted. It comes from the scores of alienated, anti-American, and politically underdeveloped kids who flooded SDS just before, and just after, the April, 1965, Vietnam march. Largely due to the influence of this group, SDS at its 1965 convention voted to remove from its constitution all anti-totalitarian (read anti-Communist) statements and agreed to continue its protests against the Vietnam war without bothering to voice substantial criticisms of the Vietcong. This was apocalyptic romanticism, and what Lenin once called "infantile leftism," but it wasn't anything as sinister as some veterans of the 1930's projected.

More recently, as a result of organizational contacts with the Trotskyites and other tribes on the Marxist-Left, SDS has become more critical of those organizations. In November of 1965 SDSers saw a Trotskyite caucus try to take over the National Coordinating Committee to End the War in Vietnam, at a convention in Washington. Later, when the May 2nd Movement dissolved, SDSers witnessed their communitarian chapters swamped by disciplined cadres of Leninists, mouthing simplistic slogans about imperialism. Also, recent upheavals in the Third World, in Algeria, Ghana, and Indonesia, have shaken some of the SDS romanticism about the anti-American *Zeitgeists* of Africa and Asia. Although a few in SDS believe these upheavals were plotted by the CIA in collusion with capitalist cartels, the majority are beginning to see the complexities of world politics—that there are few "good guys," and no simple morality plays. Most SDSers probably support Castro because of his "contact with the masses," but the other anti-colonial revolutionaries of the Third World are certainly more skeptically viewed by SDS now than a year ago.

SDS has a long and complicated prehistory going back to 1905, when Clarence Darrow, Jack London, and Upton Sinclair founded the League for Industrial Democracy. During the 1920's the LID launched a youth division called the Student League for Industrial Democracy, whose politics were Fabian socialist. At the height of the 1930's ferment, SLID merged with the Communist-penetrated National Student League to form the American Student Union. The ASU, probably the largest student-protest organization in American history, with over 20,000 members, collapsed after the Hitler-Stalin pact in 1939. After that, the reconstituted SLID remained largely a paper organization devoted to socialist education.

In 1960 the LID decided to revitalize its student department, rechristening it the Students for a Democratic Society. But it still had only a handful of members; so few in fact that no convention was held in 1961.

Meanwhile, three of the future founders of SDS (the organization dates its birth from Port Huron, not from the LID action in 1960) were attending the University of Michigan at Ann Arbor. They were balding, introspective, academic Al Haber; Tom Hayden, editor of the campus daily; and Bob Ross, a verbal, tough-minded radical, just out of Bronx High School of Science. Of the three, it was Haber who made contact with the LID, and who began to develop the ideas that were to become SDS.

In May of 1960, three months after the first sit-in, Haber organized a conference on Human Rights in the North, at Ann Arbor, attended by over 150 students, and addressed by Michael Harrington and James Farmer. It was there that many friendships between future SNCC leaders and SDS builders were cemented.

Hayden spent the summer of 1960 covering (and demonstrating at) the Democratic national convention in Los Angeles, and then visiting the New Left's cradle—Berkeley—for a month, where, according to Hayden, "I got radicalized."

Slowly, the concept of a new direct action, non-ideological national student organization began to grow, and some of the brightest young dissenters in the country became involved in the planning. Robb Burlage from Texas, a gifted economist and writer; Tim Jenkins, the student-body president at Howard University and a founder of SNCC; Gary Weisman, the student-body president of the University of Wisconsin; Tom Kahn, at twenty the author of a precocious pamphlet, *The Unfinished Revolution;* and Haber, Hayden, and Ross at Ann Arbor.

A group of about 35 met at Ann Arbor on December 28–31, 1961, to set up an SDS executive structure and agree upon a founding convention to be held the following June. It was also agreed that an SDS manifesto was to be written in preparation for the June convention by Hayden. All through the spring of 1962 Hayden sent out mimeographed drafts of the document he was working on to student and adult radicals, inviting suggestions and criticisms.

The official founding convention was held June 11–15th at the FDR Labor Center at Port Huron, Michigan. It was attended by fifty-nine individuals, including forty-three with votes, representing eleven functioning SDS chapters, or groups. There were five voting members from Ann Arbor, thirteen from New York City, three from Oberlin, three from Johns Hopkins, two from Swarthmore, and one from Earlham College. Vassar was represented by proxies. The other voting members were not from campuses, like Tim Jenkins, Bob Zellner, Jim Monsonis, and Casey Hayden, who were then associated with SNCC.

Recalling Port Huron, Ross says, "It was a little like starting a journey. We all felt very close to each other. I remember singing freedom songs all night, and Casey singing 'Hold On' so that I'll never forget it."

There was lengthy debate at the convention over the generic

definition of the *Port Huron Statement,* and finally the following resolution was adopted:

> This document represents the results of several months of writing and discussion among the membership, a draft paper, and revisions by the SDS national convention. . . . It is presented as a document with which the SDS officially identifies, but also as a living document, open to change with our times and experience. It is a beginning in our own debate and education, in our dialogue with society.

"We are people of this generation," the *Port Huron Statement* began, "bred in at least modest comfort, housed now in universities, looking uncomfortably to a world we inherit." Showing the strong influences of C. Wright Mills and Erich Fromm, the manifesto went on to support political realignment and suggest that the university was the catalytic agent of social change. It attacked the Dixiecrat-Republican alliance that then suffocated the Congress; the deterrence theory; "paranoic anti-communism"; capitalism and the welfare state; the military-industrial complex; the university concept of *in loco parentis;* the Soviet Union because of its "total suppression of organized opposition"; and America's support of totalitarian governments like those of South Africa, Spain, Nationalist China, and South Vietnam.

In its most disputed sections, the manifesto seemed to indicate that America, more than the Soviet Union, was then the main roadblock to a nuclear test-ban treaty and inspected disarmament. At one point it said:

> Our paranoia about the Soviet Union has made us incapable of achieving agreements absolutely necessary for disarmament and the preservation of peace. We are hardly able to see the possibility that the Soviet Union, though not "peace loving," may be seriously interested in disarmament.

At another point the statement asserted:

> There is Russian intransigence and evasiveness—which do not erase the fact that the Soviet Union, because of a strained economy, an expectant population, fears of Chinese potential, and interest in colonial revolution, is increasingly disposed to real disarmament with real controls. But there is, too, our own reluctance to face the uncertain world beyond the Cold War, our own shocking assumption that the risks of the present are fewer than the risks of a policy re-orientation to disarmament, our own unwillingness to face the implementation of our rhetorical commitments to peace and freedom.

The parent League for Industrial Democracy was enraged by these sections, as well as by the fact that the convention voted to seat an observer from the Progressive Youth Organizing Committee, the forerunner of the W. E. B. Du Bois Clubs; and elected Steve Max as field secretary. Max's father had been an editor on the *Worker*, and he had been a member of the Communist Labor Youth League more than five years before. But while still in his teens, Max had broken with the Communists after Hungary, the 20th Party Congress, and the defection of the Gates faction from the party. (Ironically, he now leads the most conservative faction in SDS and works for the CIO.)

After several private meetings, the LID sent SDS a memo summoning Haber and Hayden to a "hearing" on July 6th

> to discover whether or not the officers of the SDS acted, and plan to act, in accordance with the basic principles of the parent organization. Until that time no materials, manifestoes, constitutions, or other publications having to do with policy in any way, shape or form whatsoever may be mailed or distributed by the students under the identification of SDS, nor shall the LID pay for the preparation, printing and mailing or distribution of any such material.

The SDS, then less than one month old, reacted in fury and panic. The national executive committee was informed, and within twenty-four hours most of its seventeen members were in New York.

Bob Ross remembers his reaction to the LID attack was "anger." He recalls:

> We were locked out of our own office. All of us felt our future careers were going to be ruined, and America's best liberals were on the lip of red-baiting us out of existence. We knew we weren't communists, but the idea that our parent organization thought we were, was Kafkaesque.

Hayden still speaks with cold bitterness about the LID's attack. He says now:

> It taught me that Social Democrats aren't radicals and can't be trusted in a radical movement. It taught me what Social Democrats really think about civil liberties and organizational integrity.

On July 6th, from 3 to 5 P.M., with a large chunk of the SDS membership (myself included) waiting tensely in the office, Haber and Hayden, along with Tim Jenkins and Harvard graduate student Robb Burlage, confronted the LID board. The LID hierarchy then included ILGWU and Jewish Labor Committee leaders Nathaniel Minkoff, Murray Gross, Isaiah Minkoff, and Emanuel Muravchik, all veterans of trade-union faction fights with Communists. The board also included Socialist Party leaders like Michael Harrington, Samuel Friedman, and Irwin Suall.

The LID charged at the meeting that the Port Huron convention was

> unrepresentative of the organization, undemocratic in its operation and outside the basic principles of the LID in its actions.

Haber and Hayden denied this, but the LID board voted to fire the elected SDS staff, and to appoint an SDS staff representative of the LID's political viewpoint to supervise the SDS office in its day-to-day operation.

The SDS leadership met almost continuously in Steve Max's apartment through Sunday and Monday, July 8th and 9th, voting, with only one dissent and one abstention, to support Haber and Hayden and to appeal the decisions of the LID board. Present briefly at these sessions was young LID board member Andrew Norman, who, along with Norman Thomas and Dr. Harold Taylor, felt the LID had acted too hastily and too harshly. During the Monday meeting the SDS was informed that the LID had changed the lock on the SDS office, and that the office would no longer be accessible to SDS members.

For several weeks it appeared that the infant organization would collapse, or else split from the LID and try to build an independent base. But with the cross of Soviet apologist already nailed to it by the adult liberal community, that path seemed hopeless.

By August SDS had finally won most of its points, and as Ross says:

> The old socialists decided to give us the rights organized workers had won in 1938. We won the right not to be locked out of our own office and the right to honestly disagree with our boss without getting fired.

It was largely through the generous intercession of Dr. Taylor and seventy-eight-year-old Norman Thomas that SDS survived its birth trauma.

Three years later Michael Harrington, by then known as "Mr. Poverty," and the new chairman of a somewhat revitalized LID, publicly apologized to SDS for his actions during the summer of 1962.

A national student organization is a fragile thing. It has little money. Its face on each campus can be transfigured by a few graduations or a few entering freshmen. Its leaders, still in their early twenties, often find their own values and ideas vulnerable to change. The constituency a student organization must court is an emotional and fickle one, moved by peace concerns one month, an atrocity in the South the next, a book on poverty the third.

Nevertheless, SDS very slowly began to grow from the nucleus of forty-three people who met at Port Huron, and who were unified emotionally by the trouble with the LID.

In retrospect, SDS's first steps now look innocuous. It organized a liberal caucus at the NSA congress at Columbus, Ohio, at the end of the summer, and once school began, started propagandizing for campus political parties based on the models of SLATE at Berkeley and VOICE at Michigan.

During those first few months, the energy of the few fulltimers was channeled into organizing campus chapters of SDS, servicing them with speakers and an already impressive bulk of literature, like the *Port Huron Statement* and Burlage's mimeographed essay, *The South as an Underdeveloped Country*.

But once formed, these chapters were limited to campus activities: challenging conservatives to debate, fund-raising for SNCC, or deluging the campus newspaper with polemical articles.

The 1962–63 academic year saw the first wave of student protests at ebb tide. The sit-ins, freedom rides, and peace demonstrations had crested, breaking against the shoals of Kennedy charm and good intentions. Organizations like the SPU and NUT began to lose members and disintegrate. Publications folded.

The first generation of student leaders, like Chuck McDew and Tim Jenkins, were leaving the movement to marry and build careers.

When school ended in June, 1963, SDS had nine hundred dues-paying members. Many were student government leaders, campus editors, or graduate students. Many came from academic temples like Harvard, Yale, Swarthmore, and Michigan. At that point the alienation of the hipsters, romantics, and anarchists had not yet been politicized.

It was during 1963 that the American left began to rediscover poverty. Michael Harrington published *The Other America,* which reminded us of "an unconscionable amount of human suffering among 40 million poor." Dwight MacDonald wrote a twenty-eight-page essay on poverty that ran between the glittering advertisements of *The New Yorker Magazine.* Bayard Rustin preached a sermon to the SNCC convention about organizing poor whites in the North.

In April of 1963 Hayden, then SDS president, wrote a letter to UAW president Walter Reuther requesting money to finance an "education and action program around economic issues." Reuther gave SDS five thousand dollars, and that turned out to be the beginning of ERAP—the jump from the campus into the ghetto.

According to Hayden, "ERAP on paper was primarily geared towards organizing poor whites. It was only in practice that it became mostly a black movement. In Newark, for example, we had been told the Clinton Hill community was mixed, but when we got there it turned out to be all Negro." ERAP on paper was also envisaged as a series of "summer institutes." There was no expectation that hundreds of students would be so excited by the idea they would be willing to quit school and organize full-time in slum neighborhoods for a year or more.

What had happened was that by 1964 many students had already been South, and they returned North to perceive more clearly the same problems in their own backyard. Swarthmore students saw hereditary poverty and police brutality in nearby Chester, Pennsylvania, and began the first ERAP project there.

ERAP turned out to be a Pandora's box for SDS. It provided a mechanism to begin implementing the values and "participatory democracy" of the *Port Huron Statement*. It gave campus-caged and restless students a way to *act*, to *experience*, and to *confront* segregation and poverty directly. But it also generated the first deep factional cleavage in SDS, between the "ghetto jumpers" and those more concerned with the campus and the development of intellectual skills. At the beginning ERAP saw the "unspoiled poor" as *the* agency of social change, as the "surrogate proletariat." Less romantic SDSers understood the mathematics better: that all the poor, even if organized, were still a minority (20 percent) of the country, and alliances were still required with other, less revolutionary sectors of the society. During 1964 the ERAP faction, led by the charismatic Hayden, came to dominate SDS, and the "coalitionists" like Steve Max, and the "intellectuals" like Al Haber, became a besieged minority. But by the 1965 SDS convention, held at Kewadin, Michigan, equilibrium was restored by the modest achievements of the ghetto projects and by the growing fury against the war in Vietnam. Many SDSers at the 1965 convention argued that it was the middle-class professors, clergymen, and liberals who were the segment of the society most in motion, and not the desperately poor.

There are now 10 ERAP projects. Those in Chicago, Cleveland, and Appalachia are working with poor whites. In Newark; New Haven; Chester, Pennsylvania; Baltimore; Oakland; Boston; and Cairo, Illinois; the students have dug into Negro communities.

Paul Booth, who worked during the summer of 1965 on the Oakland project before he became national secretary of SDS, explains the theory behind the projects this way:

> I think real social change comes only when ordinary people get organized. Real change doesn't come from bureaucratic liberal institutions, or from legislatures. Laws always get passed, but the poor are still poor. So I think you must have some kind of thrust, an independent thrust from the grassroots, to open a dialogue with the liberals. We have to

do something that will energize the liberals. Like we had a march on Washington against the war, and seven months later SANE had one, or SNCC had a summer project in 1964, and then the SCLC had one the next summer. So maybe if we can do some successful community organizing now, it will be a spur to get King, Reuther and the churches to do the same thing themselves next year.

Life on the projects is hard. The early idealism of the volunteers has been shattered by the violence, self-hatred, apathy, and lack of unity among the underclass. Many project workers have been beaten up, and a few of the girls have been almost raped. Almost all the projects have been robbed repeatedly. Food is scarce and privacy nonexistent. Except for Newark and Chicago, the projects have had to struggle merely to endure. Lack of money, personality clashes among organizers, and red-baiting have all taken their toll.

Chicago's Uptown section looks like any other urban slum in America. The tenements are run-down, the hallways smell of urine, many windows are broken. Drunks are folded in grotesque shapes in the doorways. The garbage is uncollected, and whiskey bottles wrapped in paper bags seem to grow in every front yard. The fugue of the police siren and the ambulance wail is heard often. Unemployment is about 25 percent. But two things make Uptown different. One is that it is populated mostly by poor whites from the mountains of Kentucky and Tennessee, and the other is the shabby storefront headquarters of JOIN (Jobs or Income Now), SDS's Chicago project.

Like most of the other projects, JOIN has had its periods of growth and stagnation. In the summer of 1965 a flood of twenty-five raw volunteers almost submerged the project. But during the fall there were only four staff organizers, and fifty and sixty poor whites were turning out for meetings that discussed rent strikes, opposition to urban renewal, and ways to humanize Mayor Richard Daley's "war on poor people." The JOIN staff, like all the SDS community organizers, make no attempt to impose their ideas on the poor, but rather to learn from the poor and to nurture indigenous leadership. Although they like to think of themselves as radical organizers, sometimes ERAP workers seem more like anarchist priests than agitators; more like redeemers than revolutionists. But they are sharply aware of the danger of just becoming "a social worker with radical politics," and try to find a middle ground between that and the top-down, disciplined organizing they associate with Saul Alinsky's Industrial Areas Foundation.

ERAP workers are almost all extremely bright. Twenty-two-year-old Richie Rothstein, one of the staff members of JOIN, is a graduate of Harvard and the London School of Economics. Instead of organizing for subsistence wages he could easily be teaching political philosophy at a major university.

During the summer of 1965, Casey Hayden worked on the JOIN project. Casey, from Victoria, Texas, once married to Tom Hayden, has worked on both SNCC and SDS projects, and to many she personalizes all of the sensitive and lyrical qualities of the movement. The following is a poem she wrote while in Chicago. Its melancholy coda captures a mood many movement veterans feel.

An Organizing

To sing so others hear
and join the song
requires a silence far inside
secured by suffering
and
ease with solitude

Perhaps
the bugle calls
a whisper passed along
a sigh swiftly shared

*Perhaps
the song
is
sad.*

In Newark, the "SDS kids," as the community people call them, started the Newark Community Union Project (pronounced "encup") in the spring of 1964. It began with three white students (Carl Whitman, Tom Hayden, and Barry Kalish) going door to door in the all-Negro Clinton Hills section. The city's civil-rights commission said they were Communists. The Democratic city administration said they were there to foment riots (this just after the Harlem and Rochester explosions during the summer of 1964). Local NAACP and CORE leaders attacked them as extremists. Tom Hayden was arrested on a clearly trumped-up charge of assault. But after almost two years, NCUP's staff has grown to twenty-five, evenly divided between "SDS kids" and local Negroes. It has won slum repairs and more frequent garbage collection. It has forced "de-activation" of an urban renewal plan that would have uprooted thousands of families. It elected one of its own members, Mrs. Bessie Smith, chairman of the area board of the city's War on Poverty. It mobilized hundreds for a series of marches against police brutality. And perhaps more importantly, it has given hundreds, maybe thousands of poor Negroes, the gifts of dignity and hope.

Because of his energy and creativity, Tom Hayden is the pivot of NCUP, although he tries hard not to be the leader of the project and inevitably pleads with visiting reporters to talk to other project workers, or better yet, to the poor themselves. But still, Hayden has all the qualities of the ideal leader, and there is constant tension between his instinct and his insight. Hayden says:

> NCUP is like SNCC because we raise the question of how do people alter the condition of their life, and who should power be responsible to. We are trying to break down the

barriers to decision-making. We are saying ordinary, common people should make decisions about urban renewal and the war on poverty. But by society's standards these ordinary people in Clinton Hills are the *least* qualified to make decisions. But by insisting the poor can make decisions, we are striking at all of the society's pretense, respectability and hierarchy.

Most political ghetto movements are organized around charismatic leaders, synthetic crises and immediate demands. But we are trying to organize, first, around the feeling of being poor and powerless, rather than being black. We are also trying to organize so that poor people develop a consciousness of themselves as worthwhile human beings. Flashy demonstrations don't interest us that much.

Phil Hutchings is perhaps atypical of the ERAP worker. He seems more rooted in reality and less anti-American than most, and less bruised by his conflicts with the politicians, courts, slum lords, and police of Newark. He attended Howard University, during 1964 he worked "out of curiosity" in the Robert Kennedy campaign for the Senate. Hutchings says:

We are trying to make people think and change their values. If we talk about economic questions, it is generally just to get inside someone's home. What we're really organizing around is a sense of alienation and powerlessness. When we find a woman home every day watching a soap opera on television, we don't try to force her attention away from the TV to the rats and roaches, but we try to make her think what it is about her life that makes her watch that soap opera every day.

It is difficult to say how many people NCUP has actually organized. Several thousand receive its mimeographed newsletter; several hundred turn out for its infrequent street demonstrations; perhaps 200 community people can be considered committed and participate in block meetings and decision-making.

But Hayden understands that NCUP can only be "judged in terms of years . . . you can't expect anything quick or dramatic. We're not hung up about time."

ERAP has not yet built an "interracial movement of the poor." Probably most of the projects will not touch anyone's life outside of a small radius near their headquarters. But JOIN in Chicago is an important experiment, and NCUP might someday play a crucial role, as Newark's Negro majority inches toward political consciousness. ERAP is neither a panacea nor even a successful experiment yet. The urban poor are not easily organized, as SNCC found out in the South. It is unrealistic to expect miracles from white students organizing, in new ways, in the brutalized black ghettoes of the North. ERAP is simply a heroic beginning, nothing more.

On the 15th and 16th of October, 1965, an estimated 80,-000 persons in fifty different cities marched in protest against the war in Vietnam. The nationwide protest had been called for by the *ad hoc* Vietnam Day Committee in Berkeley and coordinated by another *ad hoc* student group in Madison, Wisconsin. But somehow the mass media got the notion SDS had triggered these demonstrations, and within two weeks *Time, Newsweek, Life,* and every television network had visited SDS's Spartan national office. Attorney General Katzenbach announced the Justice Department was investigating SDS. Senators ranging from Left to Right rose on the floor to excoriate SDS for its alleged encouragement of a movement to avoid the draft. The President added to the general attack, and to the blurring of differences between protest marches, draft-card burnings, and legal draft resistance, when press aide Bill Moyers said, "The President feels it is possible for our adversaries to misread events in this country and to take and put into these events greater and broader support for a particular position than is justified by the feeling of the American people at large."

Suddenly, SDS was receiving the greatest publicity in its history. It was being investigated, called treasonous on the Senate floor, and getting written up in almost every mass-circulation magazine. Network TV camera crews were coming in and out of the Chicago office on the hour. David Susskind was calling from New York, asking Paul Booth to appear on Open End. Scores of campuses were requesting SDS speakers. The staff in Chicago hardly slept for a week, as it ground out crisis press statements and answered the relentless ring of the telephone.

At the zenith of the hysteria, Paul Booth flew to Washington to hold a press conference in the Grand Ballroom of the National Press Club. The press came, half expecting Booth to burn his draft card for them, or else to denounce the President and Attorney General in a fiery tantrum. Instead, Booth read a statement that seemed to express the best of SDS's radicalism. It said in part:

> The commitment of SDS, and of the whole generation we represent, is clear: we are anxious to build villages; we refuse to burn them. We are anxious to help and change our country; we refuse to destroy someone else's country. We are anxious to advance the cause of democracy; we do not believe that cause can be advanced by torture and terror.
>
> We are fully prepared for service to our country and to democracy. We volunteer to go into Watts to work with the people of Watts to rebuild that neighborhood to be the kind of place that the people of Watts want it to be—and when we say "rebuild," we mean socially as well as physically. We volunteer to help the Peace Corps learn, as we have been learning in the slums and in Mississippi, how to energize the hungry and desperate and defeated of the world to make the big decisions about their own future—and to carry out those decisions. We volunteer to serve in hospitals and schools in

the slums, in the Job Corps and VISTA, in the new Teacher Corps—and to do so in such a way as to strengthen democracy at its grassroots. And in order to make our volunteering possible, we propose to the President that all those Americans who seek so vigorously to build instead of burn be given their chance to do so. We propose that he test the young people of America: if they had a free choice, would they want to burn and torture in Vietnam, or to build a democracy at home and overseas. . . .

Our generation is not afraid of service for long years and low pay: SDS has been working for years in the slums of America at $10 a week to build a movement for democracy there. We are not afraid to risk our lives—we have been risking our lives in Alabama and Mississippi, and some of us died there. But we will not bomb the people, the women and children, of another country.

Having proved its mettle in this crisis, SDS, in the last six months, has repeatedly displayed a maturing political sophistication, creatively balancing decentralization with structure, Utopianism with realism, activism with scholarship. The best qualities of SDS are surging more and more to the surface—its patient, selfless commitment to radical social change, the tough-minded intelligence of its older members, its devotion to democratic values, its flexibility in adjusting to new variables, its insights into the concentrations of power in labor, academic, and corporate bureaucracies.

Perceiving the limitations and inevitable dead end of a single-issue movement, SDS has voted to "re-emphasize" domestic issues, and "de-emphasize" its anti-war activity. (This has been hard to do in practice, since most activists see the Vietnam War as the great moral issue of their generation.) The membership decisively voted down in referendum two wholly impractical proposals: one to abolish the posts of president and national secretary, and the other to make opposition to the draft SDS's major organizational priority. SDS's national executive committee voted unanimously to protest the trial and sentencing last winter of the Soviet writers Sinyavsky and Daniel, and to express solidarity with the few Russian students who protested the trial. In Newark, NCUP became a catalytic agent in an emerging political coalition of Negro politicians, white liberal Democrats, and ghetto poor, pointed toward an assault on city hall in 1970.

SDS is still in transition, still a student group vulnerable to the vagaries of next year's freshman class and to events in Washington and Hanoi beyond its control. Facile prophecies of a glory-filled future would be foolish. Yet, a growing optimism about this guerilla band of participatory democrats suggests that only a fraction of its history is already written.

Chapter 7
The Hereditary Left

Yes, the great event of the twentieth century was the forsaking of the values of freedom by the revolutionary movement, the progressive retreat of socialism based on freedom before the attacks of Caesarism and military socialism. Since that movement a certain hope has disappeared from the world and a solitude has begun for each and every man.

—ALBERT CAMUS

■ Many of the New Left's chroniclers have depicted it as an unbroken continuum from the Peace Corps volunteers to the most doctrinaire Trotskyite tribe. This chapter is an attempt to challenge that misconception and to crystallize the crucial division between the essentially humanist and existential New Left (SNCC, SDS, SSOC, FSM) and the hereditary Marxist Left. I would contend that this fringe, centered around the Maoist Progressive Labor Party (PLP), is not a more militant extension of the New Left, but actually its opposite, whose roots are in the Old Left, and in such youth groups as the Young Communist League and the Labor Youth League. The pro-Soviet, reformist W. E. B. Du Bois Clubs are a more complicated phenomena and will be examined separately later in this chapter.

It was not an obvious choice to treat the PLP and the Hereditary Left in this fashion. PL members have exhibited authentic courage in defying restrictive travel bans and coercive grand juries. They are young people, often under twenty-one, whose phones are tapped, whose mail is checked, and whose apartments are bugged. They are treated brutally by the police and unjustly by the lower courts. The major newspapers refuse to cover them objectively. Thus there is much about PL to generate sympathy and support. But there are the legatees of Stalin and of an ideology that is violent, undemocratic, and bureaucratic.

There are a variety of ways in which groups like PL are antithetical to the mainstream of the New Left.

For one, PL believes in violence, and the New Left doesn't. When coal miners struck in Hazard, Kentucky, in 1963, and a tentative local movement developed, PL dispatched several of its leaders there with a station wagon filled with guns and Marxist pamphlets. PL had decided Hazard was a "classic situation" for guerrilla warfare. The area was surrounded by mountains. There was a reactionary local union, brutal police, and exploitive mining companies. But the PL cadre was chased out of town after it published a newspaper that informed the miners, "Objectively, you are already Communists." PL also tried to spread the 1964 Harlem riots once they got started.

Secondly, PL adheres to strict Marxist-Leninist principles. This drives it to a hair-splitting hatred of Trotskyite "devils," New Left "heretics," and the "opportunists and revisionists" of the Communist Party. Polemics are written with all the 1930's crudities about "correct ideology," "democratic centralism," "imperialist warmongers," and "capitalist lackies." Organizationally this has led PL to resemble the Communist Party of the 1930's, even though its entire leadership was either expelled from, or quit, the CP. In contrast to the loose, decentralized structure of SDS, PL has a set of bureaucratic requirements for membership. This includes a trial work period of three months and the approval of two-thirds of the local club. Additionally, PL members

> must be part of a study group in his club. . . . A member
> may not hold dual membership in organizations whose poli-
> cies are objectively counter-revolutionary. . . . Groups hav-

ing a discipline outside the party—factions and cliques—shall not be tolerated. . . . No party member may make unconstructive statements publicly about the party, gossip about other party members, or disclose confidential information to non-party members.

Where the atmosphere around SDS is informal, communitarian, and warm, PL's conspiracy-oriented militants spend considerable time in "secret meetings," disappearing "underground," infiltrating the Communist Party, dodging FBI agents, and changing their names, often more for paranoid than political purposes. Lisa Armand, for example, one of PL's leaders expelled from the CP, teaches a course at the Free University of New York (FUNY) under the pseudonym of Sue Warren.

As purist ideologues, PLers ridicule the moralism and romanticism of the New Left. They think infiltrating the Army a much more sensible tactic than burning your draft card or becoming a conscientious objector. Teaching at a university and using the job to propagandize "correct ideology" makes more sense to PL than refusing to sign a loyalty oath, as *Studies on the Left* editor Norman Fruchter recently did at Rutgers University. The moral imperatives of the anti-war groups seem self-indulgent and "bourgeois romanticism" to PL.

Like the CP of the 1930's, PL is oddly Puritanical and reactionary in cultural tastes. Where Russian Communist leader Karl Radek once called *Ulysses* "a microscope focused on a dunghill," and where the CP dismissed the creations of Eliot and Pound because of their politics, PL now attacks avant-gardists like Bob Dylan, Allen Ginsberg, and William Burroughs for their pessimism and decadence. While SDS becomes more concerned with psychological problems like depersonalization, alienation, neurosis, and spiritual *angst*, PL's ideology tells it that only economic exploitation counts. They don't understand C. Wright Mills' injunction to "translate personal problems into social issues."

Where the New Left's politics are totally a response to

domestic experience, PL's is dominated by an ideology shaped primarily by the Soviet, Chinese, and Cuban revolutions. This regenerates the 1930's notions about the creation of the "vanguard party," the endemic potential for revolution among the workers, and the belief that once "American imperialism is defeated, economic chaos will spread domestically, and the proletariat will revolt." PL sees itself as the guerrilla vanguard of this revolution. It sees its mission as increasing "revolutionary consciousness" among the workers in preparation for the collapse of capitalism. This is in contrast to the New Left, which sees capitalism as infinitely flexible and durable, and comfortably absorbing great numbers of dissenters. PL also sees American Negroes as part of the "international anti-imperialist movement." PL thus supports black nationalism, and at its 1965 convention adopted a resolution striking "the word Negro from the PL vocabulary," and replacing it with "Afro-American or black." The lead article in the March, 1965, issue of *Progressive Labor*, written by Andrew Gunder Frank, was entitled, "Black Nationalism Is the Correct Strategy."

Even the more militant members of the New Left sense the enormous difference between their values and those of the PL. Says James Weinstein, an editor of *Studies on the Left*, "The PL people are really adventurers. They get kicked out of every movement because of their extremism." Teresa del Pozzo, a former SNCC worker, says, "Those PL cats are something else. They're all hung up with discipline and cadres. They're bureaucrats with a purpose, and, man, that's the worst thing you can possibly be." SDS's former vice president Bob Ross adds, "The PL people I know are crazy and very undemocratic and all hung up on violence."

And in the June, 1965, issue of the *Realist*, Larry Cole, founder of the Lower East Side Action Project (LEAP) compared PL to the Ku Klux Klan, writing:

It is not hard to exploit hatred, whatever the philosophical cover; it is of ultimate immorality to use a man's poverty or fear as a lever of manipulation. This is equally true for those landlords who would exploit slum families for their illegitimate ends, and for PL, who would exploit the same people.

I have recently been told of PL plans to turn a peaceful demonstration against police misconduct by LEAP kids into an attack on the police. The result of such an attack would be an instant defensive retaliation against the kids. What this would bring about in a tensely integrated community is obvious. Progress, however resisted or slow, would come to a screeching halt. . . .

During its early months PL did at least share one quality with the New Left—that of bohemian freedom and a taste for experimental culture. But recently the unavoidable effects of a tightly controlled bureaucracy and CP-style Puritanism have hit PL. Marijuana smoking has been outlawed and beards ordered shaved. Couples living together have been told to marry. An approving article on Allen Ginsberg, written for the *Free Student*, the now defunct M-2-M newspaper, was killed at the last minute. So was a whimsical review of *Candy*. More and more PL members are resembling the Leninist robot Gletkin of *Darkness at Noon* and less and less do they resemble the spontaneous, feeling rebels of SDS.

The roots of PL go deep to the Communist Party of the 1950's. With the disastrous Henry Wallace campaign for the presidency in 1948, the American Communist Party started to disintegrate. In 1949 eleven of its key leaders were convicted under the Smith Act and imprisoned. The outbreak of the Korean War in June of 1950, the passage of the Internal Security Act, and the first thunderbolts of McCarthyism followed. Communists were quickly driven out of all voluntary organizations. Most of the party's dwindling resources were sapped in a struggle to defend itself against extermination by the FBI and the Justice Department. On February 25, 1956, came the revelations at the 20th Soviet Party Congress about the Stalin terror. The last God had failed. In October of 1956 came the murderous suppression of the Hungarian revolt by Soviet tanks. Within a few months a "liberal" faction inside the party, led by *Daily Worker* editor John Gates, quit. Many of the *Worker* staff and the party's last intellectuals left with Gates.

By the end of the decade the CP was a decayed skeleton. It was filled with the very old, whose emotional loyalty to the Soviet Union was the only thing they had to live for; with the children of party members who had seen their parents hunted and persecuted; and with a good number of FBI informers. The party that in 1932 had the support of Sidney Hook, Edmund Wilson, and Granville Hicks had lost all its intellectuals; all its young except for the second generation; and all its Negroes. The CP had been driven out of the CIO unions it had helped to build; it had been purged from the mainstream peace organizations under prodding from Senate investigating committees.

During the late 1950's a New York-based faction developed inside the CP that was critical of the party's cautious, reformist direction. The rebels believed the party was neither aggressive nor visible enough. They wanted the party to run its own candidates for public office and openly to recruit in the name of revolutionary Marxism. They charged the CP was following policies that "objectively supported capitalism and imperialism." They argued it was impossible to achieve a peaceful or electoral transition to "socialism" in America. They urged the party's "revisionist, class collaborationist policy" be replaced with "a revolutionary policy based on class struggle, led by a vanguard party." The dissidents also proposed that the party move its national headquarters from New York to Chicago, change its name, and "cease to be the tail to the Democratic donkey"; and that several of its key members go "underground" to begin terroristic activities "against the ruling class."

After a series of meetings the leadership of the CP turned down these proposals on the grounds that the country was still too close to the McCarthy trauma for such a strategy to have any hope of success. After the CP indirectly endorsed John F. Kennedy in 1960, the dissidents renewed their lobbying inside the party, writing vitriolic polemics.

Finally, beginning in December of 1961, the CP began to expel the "ultra-Leftists" one by one. They were accused of such sins as "dissolutionism," "adventurism," and of being "agents of the Albanian party," then the polemical euphemism for China. The CP was perceptive enough to realize the "cowardly clique" were premature Maoists. PL has since followed the lead of the Chinese on all tactical questions, from opposition to the nuclear test-ban treaty to inexplicable support of the military *coup* in Algeria to its encouragement of racist forms of nationalism.

Among the group of about 25 purged from the CP late in 1961 and early in 1962 were Milton Rosen, Mort Scheer, Fred Jerome, Sue Warren (Lisa Armand), Jake Rosen, and Bill Epton. Today these six represent the kernel of PL's unchanging leadership.

Rosen, balding, plump, and forty, is now the chairman of PL and the father figure who is asked to settle all personal problems. He had been a member of the CP's national committee and was its labor chairman for New York State. Of the split he says now, "We felt the Communist Party was no longer a revolutionary party. It had become an apologist for the liberal imperialists. . . . It supported the incorrect policy of the Meanys and the Reuthers. . . . It had become a Marxist ADA."

Scheer, thirty-nine, is the vice chairman of PL, and directs its West Coast operations. He edits the "revolutionary weekly," *Spark,* named after the Bolshevik publication Lenin founded after his split with the Mensheviks in 1903.

Epton, thirty-three and a Negro, is the Harlem chairman of PL. He came up through the Young Communist League, the Civil Rights Congress, and the CP, and is now appealing a conviction for criminal anarchy stemming from his role in the 1964 Harlem riots.

Jerome, twenty-six, is the son of the late V. J. Jerome, the CP's cultural commissar, and is named after Friedrich Engels. His brother Carl is named after Marx. Their mother, Alice, leads PL's branch on the Lower East Side in New York. Fred Jerome attended City College in New York, where he was Phi Beta Kappa and editor of the student newspaper. He joined the LYL at sixteen and the CP at twenty; before he was twenty-two the CP had expelled him. Jerome edited the magazine *Progressive Labor*, and later, the PL weekly newspaper, *Challenge*. By 1965 he was suffering from a bad ulcer, and his comrades claimed he had "gone underground."

Jake Rosen, no relation to Milton Rosen, and a college classmate of Jerome's, is also alleged by PL to be "underground." He was a college contemporary of mine, and I recall him at student meetings in the late 1950's, trying to sell Communism like a door-to-door salesman, cheerfully and aggressively. He seemed then to suffer from the occupational disease of PL: malnutrition of reality.

There is a recurring irony in the way the mass-circulation press treats PL. Having no established precedent for quickly discrediting an avowedly violent and Communist organization, the newspapers simply restate the fact that PL's leaders all come out of the Communist Party, and that therefore PL must be like the CP. In fact, however, the sectarian rivalry between PL and the CP is, of course, fierce. They are about as close politically as the Black Muslims and the NAACP. The PL publications never pass up a chance to damn the Soviet Union for its "counter-revolutionary policies," while CP leader Gus Hall has characterized PL members as "parasites on the body of the Negro freedom movement," and has publicly alleged they are being subsidized by China, through Cuba.

In short, the CP believes in coexistence with liberals, in reformist, nonviolent tactics, and follows the Soviet Union's policy of peaceful coexistence, including support of the nuclear test-ban treaty and a negotiated settlement in Vietnam. PL, meanwhile, believes liberals and labor "are the true class enemy." Rejecting coalition with such "opportunists" PL urges "militant class struggle with any means possible." And rejecting the peaceful coexistence formula, PL "supports all wars of national liberation," including a Vietcong victory in Vietnam, and hails China's decision not to sign the nuclear test-ban treaty as "courageous."

The chief architects of PL—Rosen the ideologue; Scheer the organizer; Jerome the propagandist; and Epton the Negro—met regularly through the early months of 1962. By then the peace and integration movements were beginning to gain strength. The Sino-Soviet rift was growing deeper. The American CP was continuing its cautious policies and curious purges. These events helped point the quartet to the conclusion that the moment was ripe for the creation of a Marxist-Leninist vanguard party that could represent the Chinese point of view on the American Left.

They began with the publication of *Progressive Labor* in March of 1962. The monthly magazine was then almost exclusively devoted to labor articles: attacks on Walter Reuther, reports on internal union factional fights, exposés of the AFL-CIO's "imperialist foreign policy," analysis of "sell-out contracts." Then on July 1, 1962, the Progressive Labor Movement was founded at the Hotel Diplomat in Manhattan. The meeting was attended by about 50 persons. A fourteen-member coordinating committee was set up with Rosen as its chairman, and all its participants former members of the CP.

By the middle of 1964 PL had grown to about 600 deeply committed members. While the hierarchy remained static, the base was like a revolving door, with new recruits joining, going through a brief spasm of intense militance, and then quitting in disillusionment with the disciplined structure, or the sectarianism that made "male chauvinism" synonymous with "counter-revolution," or *Studies on the Left* editors "opportunists." But at the same time PL was doing hard, day-to-day organizing work in the slums. It wasn't the mystical participatory democracy of the SDS workers, though. It was picket lines against police brutality that often led to violence, and the funneling of "Afro-American workers" into Marxist study groups. About a quarter of the PL membership was made up of working-class and minority-group people.

PL was able to recruit on the campuses partly because this was a period of general upsurge in radicalism, and even Jehovah's Witnesses could have recruited if they had an anti-American program. But PL grew also because it projected an image of fearless militance. Its organizers said openly and aggressively that they were Communists, and so what. They also gained a certain respect by defying Government authority in sponsoring two illegal student trips to Cuba, and then triggering a brawl when the trip's organizers appeared before HUAC. PL was also successful in setting up an "anti-imperialist" peace group—the May 2nd Movement—which they effectively controlled at the national level, although on some campuses like Harvard, M-2-M became an umbrella for all anti-war activity, encompassing liberals and SDSers. And the magazine, *Progressive Labor,* branched out into peace, civil-rights, and foreign-policy areas, growing to have a circulation of 6,500 under Jerome's editorship, which synthesized Leninist theory with *New York Daily News* practice.

During the fall of 1964 I got to know PL fairly well in the course of writing several articles for *The Village Voice.* Already the absence of internal democracy, a belief in violence, and mechanistic adherence to the Chinese position stamped PL as part of the Hereditary Left. But there was still a freewheeling individualism inside the organization that reflected the mood of this generation of freedom-searching rebels. It was only later that this Wobbly spirit was exorcised. Some disagreement was at first permitted within the framework of "democratic centralism." The debate over bohemianism was just beginning. Members talked candidly with the press and with members of other radical groups. The FBI was joked about. East Village poet and eccentric Marc Schleifer was one of the leaders of M-2-M. About 50 of PL's members had been recruited on the trips to Cuba, and these rebels were more in tune with the communitarian spirit and intuitive radicalism of *Fidelismo* than with stuffy Marxism-Leninism. But by 1966 the mood of PL had become secretive and somewhat paranoid. Personal behavior fell under the control of the leadership. No leader or member of the organization would let me interview him. All the bearded, hip prototypes of Fidel had left PL, or had been steeled into rigid Gletkins.

But back in 1964, before Bill Epton's conviction for criminal anarchy, and before Phillip Luce was purged from the movement, there was still some openness and candor.

During several lengthy interviews in October of 1964, Fred Jerome sketched PL's political strategy for revolution. He spoke of "the more advanced sections of the labor movement, like the Teamsters and the old CIO unions," breaking with the AFL-CIO and beginning a "more revolutionary organization." He predicted "Southern blacks will start defense clubs and reject the nonviolence of Martin Luther King." He added, "The armed Afro-Americans inside the great ghettoes, too, were ready for revolution." These three groupings, Jerome predicted, would be the leverage points for revolt, "within a very few years." His dialectical optimism grew, Jerome said, from his conviction that America was losing imperialist profits in the Third World, and this, coupled with rising automation at home, "would increase the unemployment rate rapidly."

Jerome is typical of PL's leadership. Both he and his parents were Communist Party members. After graduating from college in 1960, Jerome spent almost a year in Cuba, an event he terms "the most crucial of my political development. . . . It convinced me revolution was an actual possibility. It restored my faith."

After his return from Cuba, Jerome secured—and lost—several journalistic jobs. He worked on an Atlanta newspaper under the name of Fred Reed, but was fired for participating in civil-rights demonstrations. He worked in the makeup department of a national news magazine, but quit. Later, an FBI visit cost him a job as editor of a union newspaper in New York. After that experience, Jerome says, he abandoned all hope of success as a journalist

159

in the "capitalist world," and in early 1962 he became the full-time editor of *Progressive Labor*.

Jerome's personality is not that of the true believer. His gentle and reflective manner provides an arresting counterpoint to his often unreal, mechanistic thinking. Pausing a long while before answering questions in a distracted monotone, Jerome calls to mind Rhodesian Prime Minister Ian Smith, whose soft-sell style lends an eerie credibility to his racist slogans. So it is that Jerome, talking softly, looking right at you, can sound reasonable asserting that America is building up West Germany for a surprise attack on the Soviet Union, or that there is "fundamentally no difference between Walter Reuther and Barry Goldwater," or, "Of course the CIA had Kennedy assassinated," or "When America invaded North Korea. . . ."

Poet, writer, and critic Marc Schleifer represented the Wobbly spirit now gone from PL. Schleifer, editor of *Negroes with Guns*, left for Jerusalem in May of 1965 after being "exposed" as an "extremist" by a state legislative committee probing "subversive influence" in the anti-poverty program, Mobilization for Youth.

Schleifer, who mixes Camp and Hip with his quite brilliant Marxism, eagerly admitted during an interview, "Sure I'm a communist. In fact, I'm left of anything that exists in the world today. I'm left of Mao. To me, Khrushchev symbolizes the white liberal. Right now I'm only interested in what comes *after* communism."

Schleifer, a Jew turned Moslem, a royalist turned revolutionist, a Madison Avenue publicist turned underground man, was probably too much of an individualist for comrades addicted to "correct ideology" and cadre discipline.

He said he thought drugs and sexual freedom "were the keys to human emancipation." His favorite radicals, he said, were Allen Ginsberg, Irving Rosenthal, the editor of the now defunct little magazine, *Big Table*, and Jack Smith, the director of *Flaming Creatures*, an underground film that features glimpses of limp penises, bouncing breasts, masturbation, and oral sexuality. All of which PL would probably call symptoms of capitalist decadence.

Two events helped break down whatever individualism and openness existed in PL.

The first was the organization's role in the Harlem riots, which led to the indictment of Epton, the grand-jury harassment of PL, and the disclosure that a Negro detective, Alphonse Hart, had successfully infiltrated the group.

As even such a conservative source as the FBI confirmed, the riots were caused, at bottom, by the poverty and social decay of the ghetto. What triggered them was the fatal shooting of a fifteen-year-old Negro schoolboy, James Powell, on July 16, 1964, by an off-duty police officer named Thomas Gilligan. It seems clear, however, that once the rioting began on July 18th, PL did everything in its limited power to keep it going.

Epton told a street-corner crowd in Harlem during the rioting:

> We will not be fully free until we smash this state completely . . . in that process, we're going to have to kill a lot of cops, a lot of these judges, and we'll have to go up against their army.

During the rioting *Challenge* printed an editorial that proclaimed:

> There is no lawful government in this country today. Only a revolution will establish one. If that is "civil rebellion," let us make the most of it. . . . And when Murphy's uniformed goons attack the crowd with gas and guns, let us not run and let us not pray—let us fight back.

PL's Harlem front group, the Harlem Defense Committee, printed and distributed leaflets providing instructions for the making of Molotov cocktails. The HDC also distributed the celebrated poster with a picture of Lieutenant Gilligan over the caption: "Wanted for Murder."

After the riots the *National Guardian* quoted Milton Rosen as saying:

> We were not prepared for that historic moment [the riot]. . . . All we managed to do, aside from refusing to join in with the chorus of those so-called leaders who tried to convince the people of Harlem to clear the streets for "Bull" Murphy's police force, and trying to organize a protest march, was to print and distribute the "murder" poster. . . . We alone did not abdicate leadership during the riots. . . .

On the sixth day, after the rioting had finally subsided, Epton called for a protest march down Lenox Avenue. Every other Harlem leader, including the Black Muslims and rent-strike organizer Jesse Gray, warned such a march could only ignite bloodshed. The city obtained a restraining order. Epton called for thousands to join his protest, but only a handful showed up. Epton was jailed.

Together, these events managed to convince the panicked city administration that PL was a menace beyond its meager numbers and had to be crushed. Epton was indicted on August 5th for criminal anarchy and for advocating "overthrow of the organized government of the state of New York by force and violence." Within six months an all-white grand jury, impaneled to investigate the riots, subpoenaed more than 30 people, almost all of them connected with either PL, M-2-M, or the Student Committee for Travel to Cuba. With typical ineptness, the panel also subpoenaed one SNCC worker who was in Mississippi during the rioting.

All those summoned before the grand jury were guaranteed immunity from prosecution, which meant that if they refused to testify they were liable to contempt citations. The grand jury seemed determined to prove PL responsible for the rioting, even through the FBI report, released on September 26th, concluded the riot "was a senseless attack on all constituted authority without direct purpose or object. . . . There was no systematic planning or organization."

By early in 1965 almost a dozen PL members had been cited for contempt of the grand jury. One of them, Elinor Goldstein, a City College co-ed, was sentenced to three days in the infamous Women's House of Detention in Greenwich Village, and this created a civic uproar.

Miss Goldstein's attorney, Martin Garbus, tells the story of how he pleaded with his client on a Monday not to "play martyr," and to testify before the grand jury.

> She told me she would let me know by Wednesday what she would do. But the trouble with PL is that decisions that should be made by lawyers are made by the leaders of PL. And those leaders were willing to have the law serve their own purpose. They cared about publicity and not about their own people. . . . So on Tuesday, while I was waiting for an answer from Elinor, I got a call from the district attorney's office. And they told me they had bugged a conversation the night before, during which the PL leadership had told Elinor to go to jail, and not talk to the grand jury.

One of the friendly witnesses before the grand jury was detective Alphonse Hart, who had effectively infiltrated the PL leadership. He played a tape recording made during the riots. On the tape Epton urged the murder of "cops and judges."

According to an assistant district attorney, "Epton damn near fainted when he saw Hart was a detective. He had trusted him completely."

On December 20, 1965, a jury found Epton guilty of conspiring to riot and conspiring to overthrow the state—on the basis of a law passed in 1901 and not invoked in forty-five years.

PL's activities during the riots were clearly irresponsible and provocative. Their strategy was apparently to sustain and spread the rioting, thinking The Revolution was at hand. And the city has tried to use PL's stupidity and addiction to violence as a crowbar to break the organization, by jailing its leaders, draining its treasury, and intimidating its young members. Unfortunately, the city has only fed the fanaticism of PL, driving it even further into a Marxist-Leninist fantasy world.

In the labyrinth of the revolutionary Left, twenty-eight-year-old Philip Abbott Luce was a personality. Students recognized him by his boots, his swagger, and his red handlebar moustache. They guffawed when he called a member of HUAC "stupid, irrelevant, irrational and absolutely obnoxious." They remembered his "free speech" fight with the administration of Ohio State University, and his organizing of the two student trips to Cuba. They talked about his participation in a Times Square brawl, which erupted when police tried to break up one of the first protests against the war in Vietnam.

Luce possessed all those colorful, scene-making qualities cherished on the bohemian fringes of the Left. When the fifty-nine students returned from Cuba, Luce was their truculent spokesman before the forest of television and newsreel cameras. When a group of ten students testified before HUAC, Luce stood in the marble hallway, reading their angry manifesto.

Suddenly, in March of 1965, PL mailed press releases to every daily newspaper in New York City, revealing that Luce had been purged. He was accused of being an FBI informer, a drug addict, and of other crimes, including writing an article for the right-wing *National Review*. The release read in part:

"Philip Luce surrendered first his body, and then his soul out of mortal fear of imprisonment. . . . Sinking to the absolute depths of depravity, Luce has concocted a fantastic tale of fabrication—at the prodding of police officials—even involving several persons with whom he had been intimate friends for years."

The gist of the PL indictment was that Luce, facing twenty years in jail for a variety of revolutionary deeds, became frightened and offered to become an FBI informer. Further, the PL alleged that Luce had become a "heroin addict," and that he needed the Government's money to sustain his habit.

Luce, still claiming to be "a radical," countered by saying he had actually quit PL six weeks before, and that the public attack on him was motivated by a desire to quash dissent within the organization. "They're trying to make an example of me," he said, "and in that way intimidate anyone else who wants to quit."

Although the alleged piece for the *National Review* never appeared, Luce did write an article for *The Saturday Evening Post*, called "Why I Quit the Extreme Left," in the May 8, 1965, issue.

In the article Luce, who had been editor of PL's magazine and one of its most visible public spokesmen, charged his recent comrades with storing guns, practicing karate, organizing front groups like M-2-M and manipulating their members.

Luce says he became a "secret member" of PL in 1964, but because PL wanted to maintain "the fiction" that the Student Committee for Travel to Cuba was not dominated by PL, his membership was not disclosed until later. Documenting how M-2-M was set up as a PL front, he wrote:

We set up the national executive committee of M-2-M in such a way that Progressive Labor controlled it from its inception. At present a majority of the national controlling body of 12 are members of PL. But, as with the Student Committee for Travel to Cuba, most of the PL members on the national governing body of M-2-M are kept "secret" members.

Of the hierarchal decision-making in PL, Luce wrote:

As I worked for Progressive Labor and closely observed its leadership, I rapidly discovered that one element in the organization was making decisions and taking actions of which the rank and file had no knowledge . . . last fall I learned that without the knowledge of most members a small group had conducted extensive target practice on Long Island. . . . Then I discovered two other things—unknown to all but a few members—which made me leave PL. . . . The first was that PL has a secret arms cache in New York City, presumably to be used by a special group in terroristic activity. My second discovery concerned PL's plans to create just such a special group. In December (1964) I was invited to join a small number of the members—about 10—who would train to "go underground"—that is, to shed their present identities, leave home and family, and take on totally new identities. . . .

Much of this sounds James Bondish, and since Luce has subsequently become a cooperative witness before HUAC in executive session, and was a prosecution witness during the trial of his co-organizers of the Cuban trip, the possibility of exaggeration is great.

The point is that PL has reacted to the Luce episode in classic Stalinist fashion. In the December, 1965, issue of *Progressive Labor*, Roger Taus describes Luce as a

terrified junky who fell apart under pressure, and sold one ball to the *Saturday Evening Post*, the other to the *National Review*, his ass to the FBI, and who now appears as a screaming faggot, "spying" on public demonstrations. . . .

The same issue of *Progressive Labor* contains the following Orwellian letter to the editor:

To the Editor:
A year ago, when the dirty police agent Luce was editor of *Progressive Labor*, he published some fascist-like verses in your columns. I wrote a letter of protest, attacking the editor's motivations in publishing them.

Luce performed radical surgery on my letter. He cut out the heart of my argument against such writing and, of course, all reference to his own vile role as a slanderer of the working class and Marxism-Leninism, in having chosen to include the verses I attacked. . . .

The W. E. B. Du Bois Clubs, named after the great Negro scholar and founder of the NAACP, who became a Communist at age ninety-three, are a unique student group, and can be understood only in the context of the de-Stalinization of the Soviet Union and the steady growth of the New Left.

A generation ago the Soviet Union was the center of all revolutionary ideology and activity in the world, and the CP its domestic agent. But this is no longer true; when PL calls the CP reformist it is right. The underlying philosophy of the CP is more conservative than SNCC's or SDS's. The CP is for all the economic reforms the New Radicals scorn as tokenism and welfare colonialism—medical care for the aged, more public housing, higher minimum wage laws, and the rest. *The CP does not have a radical critique of American institutions* or of the bureaucratic, depersonalized administration of liberal programs. As Milton Rosen has said, the CP is the "Marxist ADA."

A parallel change has taken place in foreign affairs. For the last several years the Soviet Union has, more or less, followed a peaceful policy in its relations to other countries. It played an authentic peacemaking role in the India-Pakistan dispute early in 1966. The Soviet Union has become a stabilizing influence in the world, not a revolutionary one. This is a disorienting reality for many people; the New Radicals could only laugh when *Newsweek Magazine* printed a chart of the New Left that placed the CP and the Du Bois Clubs far to the left of SNCC and SDS.

Just as PL reflects many of the qualities commonly attributed to China—paranoia, fanaticism, racism, dogmatism—so do the Du Bois Clubs mirror the qualities of the Soviet Union—moderation, stability, and bureaucratic "socialism."

Although they deny it, the Du Bois Clubs are viewed as the youth wing of the Communist Party—by everyone from PL to the FBI. They are not as tightly controlled as prior CP youth groups and they permit non-Communists in the leadership—but still, there seems to be effective control by the party, and on no major question do the clubs and the party disagree.

The Du Bois Clubs, founded in San Francisco in June of 1964, have about 1500 members, heavily concentrated in the Bay area of San Francisco and in New York City. As part of the Hereditary Left, their leadership is dominated by the children of Communists. There is Bettina Aptheker, daughter of Herbert Aptheker, as well as the offspring of Eugene Dennis, Vincent Hallinan, James Forest, Saul Wachter, Roscoe Prochter, and others. Talking even to rank and file Du Bois Clubs members, and reading the group's monthly magazine, *Insurgent*, one is struck by how little they have internalized the values of the New Radicals.

Du Bois members are just not "hung-up" by the same things SDSers are. They don't talk about feeling powerless against managerial bureaucracies. They don't make embarrassing speeches about how we must love each other. They are not viscerally outraged by the moral deceits of society in the way SDS members are; they are not in total rebellion. The key difference is that Du Bois Club members don't hate their fathers; SDSers do.

The Du Bois Clubs, despite their reformist outlook, call themselves Marxist (not Leninist) and socialist, the same way the CP does. This theoretical base leads them into pro-labor, pro-working class positions, which in turn leads them to support the liberal wing of the Democratic Party. Thus, while SDSers are spontaneously outraged at the labor movement and have memorized all its crimes, from not endorsing the 1963 March on Washington to being more hawklike than the President about Vietnam, Du Bois Club members continue to abstain from attacking the AFL-CIO leadership. This kind of knee-jerk Marxism runs so deep in the organization that *Insurgent* implied that Bob Dylan had abandoned protest for "folk rock" because of pressure for profits from Columbia Records. And their working class-Democratic Party orientation led the clubs to formally endorse capitalist reformer William F. Ryan in the 1965 New York City Democratic Party primary. If SNCC views the world with the eyes of the victim, and PL sees the world through the eyes of Mao, then the Du Bois Clubs perceive the world through the eyes of the Communist Party *circa* 1934. Then the labor movement and the New Deal Democrats were the agencies of change—and events were proving Marxist analysis of capitalism accurate. But such a view makes the Du Bois Clubs an anachronism today, pro-labor, pro-Russia, and pro-Democratic Party at a time when the New Radicals consider all three conservative, worn out, and hierarchies out of touch with the people.

As the heart of the Hereditary Left, the Du Bois Clubs and PL share several similarities. Both are ideologically and organizationally disciplined; both would challenge Tom Hayden's suggestion in *The New Republic* that the New Radicals should rely "more on feel than theory." Both are also externally oriented and have existing models for social change in China and the Soviet Union. Both ignore the spiritual problems—like boredom, violence, and repression—that haunt SDSers. Both cling to the single Marxist agency of change—the proletariat—and the belief that only economic grievances can energize the workers.

But there is a great difference in the way PL and the Du Bois Clubs try to raise the consciousness of the working class to revolutionary pitch. PL believes the workers should be agitated to struggle for reforms, but that consciousness is built by the *failure* of these reform movements, not by their success. Failure, PL thinks, teaches the workers "the true, fascist character of the American ruling class," and therefore that revolution is the only possible solution. For PL, for a rent strike to fail is better than for

it to succeed; for a demonstration to be broken up by police brutality is considered a tactical triumph; for the war in Vietnam to
end would be a disaster; for it to escalate would be preferable.
(Hence, PL opposes negotiations as a demand for the peace
movement.) This defeatist strategy, when it was followed by the
Trotskyites in the past was known as "the worse the better theory of change."

Assuming that peaceful, piecemeal reform is to its disadvantage,
PL directs much of its ideological fire at liberals and moderate
radicals. Thus the following in the December, 1965, issue of *Progressive Labor:*

> Norman Thomas and Co. have set up a new campus peace
> organization. This transparent maneuver is called "Ameri-
> cans for the Reappraisal of Far Eastern Policy." These advo-
> cates of "democracy" who hurl around "slick" terms like
> "Stalinist" and "Stalinoid" expose themselves as the real bu-
> reaucrats and outside agents of the ruling class. They seek to
> impose their rule on the peace movement by hook or crook.
>
> Paradoxically, U.S. Communist Party leaders play right
> into their hands with their own phony apologies for Johnson
> as "the lesser evil fighting the ultra-right," and endorse the
> same incorrect "coalition" tactics within the Democratic
> Party as the previously mentioned charlatans.

As for the radical, C. Wright Millsish quarterly, *Studies on the
Left,* the PL organ says:

> In as much as the editors of *Studies* do not claim to be
> Marxist-Leninists, it would be absurd to characterize them
> as revisionists, opportunists, etc. However, some of their
> concepts do parallel the thinking of right-wingers past and
> present. . . .

The Du Bois Clubs, however, consider reform victories with
capitalist allies crucial to the development of consciousness and to

combating the apathy and cynicism of the workers. Thus, the clubs' political program is almost indistinguishable from that of the liberal-Social Democratic LID. It advocates a broad coalition of liberal forces like trade unions and civil-rights groups working in harness with the Democratic Party. The clubs do not support violence, and are uneasy with some of the more experimental forms of protest devised by SNCC and SDS. Unlike any of the other student groups, the Du Bois Clubs place continued stress on the threat from the ultra-Right. They see the political spectrum much more clearly than does even SDS. The Du Bois Clubs do not attack Walter Reuther as a "sell-out" or Hubert Humphrey as an accomplice to imperialism in the Dominican Republic. The clubs, perhaps due to the persecution of the Communist Party, have not lost sight of the influence of the Goldwater Right, or the Dodd-style anti-Communists. In meetings with other organizations, Du Bois Club activists tend to advocate the strategy of forgetting sectarian differences and uniting to fight the right-wing and big business. And usually SDSers, who see "corporate liberalism" as the immediate enemy, hoot the Du Bois activists down and suggest they join the Young Democrats.

The founding convention of the clubs, June 19–21, 1964, was a riotous affair, punctuated by fist fights and climaxed by a walkout by PL, the Trotskyites, and independent radicals.

The convention was billed as the start of "a new nation-wide socialist youth organization," and an assortment of dissenters showed up. They were greeted by a five-point program that included support of "peaceful co-existence and disarmament," and asserted, "It is the working people of the country . . . who will ultimately be the decisive force meeting our pressing social and economic needs." It went on to state:

"The greatest danger to American democracy comes from the racist and right-wing forces acting in alliance with the most reactionary sections of the economic power structure."

The reformist manifesto didn't satisfy the PL and Trotskyite delegations. They wanted an open avowal of socialism and condemnation of the liberals, and managed to get to the floor a resolution attacking the then Attorney General Robert Kennedy.

As quoted by Richard Armstrong in *The Saturday Evening Post*, a PL delegate commented, "It was surrealistic. We told them, man, this cat Kennedy wants to put you in jail. But they wouldn't even listen." The resolution was defeated 229 to 202, but on a complicated weighted-vote formula that was clearly rigged to favor the Du Bois Club cadres, which never intended the convention to be an open one.

A few months later, PL's theoretical organ, the *Marxist Leninist Quarterly*, published a shrill attack on the Du Bois convention, penned, ironically, by Philip Luce prior to his purge and conversion to HUAC. Luce wrote:

> This so-called socialist youth conference ended with a program that made it a bit more moderate than the ADA. . . .
> To simply allow the opportunists [Du Bois Clubs] to send these potential militants into the present mass organizations to be stultified and reduced to robots of the Democratic Party is impossible and unthinkable. We must develop a logical, revolutionary policy that will show these young people that we have a viable alternative to supporting the Democratic Party or CORE or the AFL-CIO. . . . We must declare an unremitting war against the opportunists in the American socialist camp. Sheer opportunism is as evil as the racist, imperialist policies of the American government and must be fought as adamantly. . . .

Although I have several close friends in SDS and SNCC, I have none in the Du Bois Clubs. This has meant I have only been able to observe club members in formal, pre-set situations, like meetings and interviews. I have not had the benefit of relaxed, candid conversations with friends in the organization, and I have not had the opportunity to engage club members in a variety of spontaneous settings. In impersonal interviews I have sensed that Du Bois members have self-consciously tried to persuade me they are not related to the Communist Party and are a genuine section of the New Left. So the following are some impressionistic notions I have developed about the Du Bois membership, which are the product of information as well as intuition.

Some of the club members—mostly the younger recruits—can almost be mistaken for somewhat square New Left types. They work selflessly in community organizing. They participate actively in the anti-war movement, generally advocating a moderate negotiations position rather than immediate withdrawal of American troops. They were active in the leadership of the FSM. Du Bois activists also participate in political campaigns when a "progressive" candidate is running. This segment of the membership—possibly a quarter—is neither Marxist nor socialist—but seems more like the left-wing of the Young Democrats. These members are attracted by the clubs' moderate program of piecemeal reform, by the slogans of unity against the right-wing, and by the earnestness of the leadership. It is the presence of such ordinary Left liberals that makes the clubs unlike any prior Communist youth movement, and indicates that even the CP perceives that this generation of rebels cannot be converted into robots.

The rest of the clubs' members—who also work on reformist projects—are Marxists, the children of "progressive parents," and sympathetic to the Soviet Union, although they do not worship it blindly the way the 1930's Communists did.

These members are almost totally bereft of that distinctive style and tone that helps define the New Left as heirs of the anarchists and the Beats. For one, this majority of Du Bois activists are the reverse of bohemian, and, as presumed Communists, almost manic in their urge to be respectable. They dress like workers rather than in the shaggy beard-black stockings-Beatle cap costume of the Beats. Almost no one smokes marijuana. At parties they listen to Woodie Guthrie or Pete Seeger records, rather than to Bob Dylan or the Lovin' Spoonful. It seems as if these youths are completely untouched by the influence of the Beats, and are

173

the direct descendants of Earl Browder and the Progressive Party. Disciplined and middle class, they lack the churning anger and total rebellion (not just political) of the SNCC and SDS types. They also appear unable to understand the New Left's romantic and visionary drive for "community"; perhaps the ideal of the Soviet Union fills that emotional void for them. It is as if these Du Bois members inherited their politics rather than absorbing them through painful conflict with their environment. In their guts they don't *feel* repressed and dehumanized by a managerial society. Lacking the bottom-up, anti-leader mystique of the New Left, they are potential bureaucrats themselves.

Intellectually, most of the clubs' leaders seem much inferior to those in SDS and SNCC. They are mechanical and uncreative in their thinking, and seem dependent on their memorized and vulgarized Marxism for understanding: hence, Dylan goes rock because the capitalists at Columbia Records told him to. Most of the Du Bois leaders think America is in Vietnam for only imperialistic motives, but once they recite a few paragraphs from Lenin's "Imperialism, the Last Stage of Capitalism," they appear unable to cope with the suggestion that wars may be caused by irrational reasons rooted in human nature or by noneconomic reasons like nationalism.

Yet, unlike PL, the Du Bois leaders are sensitive about their Soviet Marxism, and try hard to give it a 4-H American gloss. Their magazine, *Insurgent*, recently featured an interview with the Beatles' Paul McCartney. Although their speech has been infiltrated with words like "workers" and "class struggle" and "progressive," Du Bois leaders avoid all sectarian attacks on other groups on the Left, even PL. And although they don't really do it, they talk about being creative in their Marxism, and applying it experimentally to the American experience. There is almost a tragic quality to their desire to be part of the New Left, while their Old Left style keeps them alien to the intuitive swingers of SNCC and SDS. It's a little like watching a middle-aged matron in a corset trying to do the frug.

Chapter 8
The Generation Gap

Come mothers and fathers throughout the land,
And don't criticize what you can't understand.
Your old road is rapidly aging.
Please get out of the new one if you can't lend a hand,
For the times, they are a-changin'.

—BOB DYLAN

It is hard to hear a new voice, as hard as it is to listen to an unknown language.

—D. H. LAWRENCE

You can't trust anyone over 30.

—FSM SLOGAN

■ Generational conflict is inevitable when a younger, insurgent generation creates its own movement and ethos. Today such conflict is taking place in almost all the arts. In jazz, there are angry, nationalistic pioneers like Cecil Taylor and Archie Schepp challenging the harmonic orthodoxies of Count Basie and Dizzy Gillespie. In film, there is a Dadaist experimental movement led by Jonas Mekas, which is mocked by the above-ground technicians, and, in turn, defended by young critic Susan Sontag. In the theater a new generation, influenced by Luigi Pirandello and Antonin Artaud, has produced the Living Theatre and the dramas of Jack Gelber and Kenneth Brown. In literature, an under-thirty-five faction of black humorists including Thomas Pynchon and John Barth is in conflict with older, more rationalistic critics. Even in popular music, Bob Dylan and the folk rockers, all under thirty years of age, now speak to a new generation, and are effectively challenging the sentimental hegemony of Pat Boone and Ricky Nelson.

The best of the SDS organizers are asking the same questions as Dylan in "Desolation Row," Pynchon in *V*, and Allen Ginsberg in *Howl*. What is sane and what is insane? What is legal and what is illegal? What does it mean to be "qualified," and who decides? It is all one generation's revolt against the last one's definitions of reality.

So it should not be surprising that one of the difficulties afflicting the New Radicalism is that it is cut off from the older leaders and traditions of American dissent. And since the stated goal of both generations is to create a genuine Left opposition—something which does not now exist—this estrangement is to be lamented, although sectarians of each generation have celebrated it as confirmation of their own monopoly of radical wisdom.

The reasons for the discontinuity of radical generations are plentiful and understandable. Some are the irrational psychological consequences of generational loyalties. But enough are political and programmatic so that eighty-one-year-old pacifist A. J. Muste can become a patron of the New Left, while twenty-seven-year-old Tom Kahn of the Fabian LID can become a strident critic.

The New Radicalism is authentically new in its vague weaving together of anarchist, existential, transcendental, Populist, socialist, and bohemian strands of thought. *It is not the logical outgrowth of the older radical traditions in the West.* It is not built upon the same discontents as the Old Left—the depression and the threat of fascism—but upon newer discontents like powerlessness, moral disaffection, the purposelessness of middle-class life—all of which are the special products of an abundant, technocratic urban culture.

Also, America missed a whole generation of radicals that should have matured during the 1950's, but was aborted by McCarthyism, apparent prosperity, and the Cold War. In that intervening decade many things changed at an extraordinary velocity. International Communism became polycentric. Five nations were moving toward admission to the nuclear club. Humanist values slowly began to seep through the Iron Curtain. Nationalistic anti-colonial revolutions were convulsing three continents. The American labor movement completed its ossification into a conservative oligarchy. Radicals, divided by two decades, responded differently to all these events.

In the interest of simplicity I have broken the adult Left down into four broad groupings.

One group consists of ex-radicals, now pro-Cold War liberals like Sidney Hook and Lewis Feuer. They see little of value in the New Radicalism and tend to dismiss it in terms of adolescent rebellion against father figures. These Great Society liberals think America no longer requires major social reforms; only minor technical adjustments that can be made at the top of the society without chaotic upheaval at the bottom. In recoil from the lawlessness of Totalitarianism (for them it always had a capital T), they have made a fetish of law and order.

The second group consists of the Social Democratic Left, represented by Irving Howe and Bayard Rustin. These men, anti-Communist Socialists, share many objectives with the students. But they candidly criticize the New Radicalism for not being sufficiently anti-Communist, for not being reflective enough, for being too romantic, and for its emotional anti-Establishmentarianism. Their sometimes valid criticisms of the New Left have generated considerable rancor because of the polemical style of their delivery. The soft, Emersonian New Radicals do not know how to deal with rationalistic, Talmudic intellectuals trained in the *Partisan Review*-Stalinist guerrilla rumbles of the 1930's. This difference in style and tone has exacerbated the political disagreements, which in reality are not that great.

The third group of over-thirty radicals I call the Romantic Left. They have romanticized the movement's strength and have popularized its most questionable modes of thinking. As a sample of this tendency I have selected Yale professor and super-hero of the New Left, Staughton Lynd.

179

Finally, there is a fourth type of adult leftist, whom I call the Humanist Liberals. Unlike the Social Democrats, they are not theoretical Marxists but improvisational pragmatists, and not nearly as anti-Communist. Unlike the Romantic Left, they are neither violently anti-American nor beguiled by visions of the apocalypse. Represented by muckraking journalist I. F. Stone and writer Arthur Waskow of the influential Institute for Policy Studies, this group has been deeply affected by the New Radicalism, but has retained enough of its own rationalistic identity to see the flaws of the new movements with piercing clarity.

From the mountain top of revolutionary true belief there descends a slippery slope that leads to the parched wasteland of Jay Lovestone and all the ex-Stalinists who became HUAC informers. Others have quit the mountain top and found honorable crevices high on the radical slope; men like Ignazio Silone and Murray Kempton among them. Still others, once they lost their iron grip on the peak, tumbled to the Messianic style of anti-Communism symbolized by *The New Leader*. It is to that valley that Hook and Feuer have fallen from the summit of their faith in the dictatorship of the proletariat.

The Hook-Feuer school of former radicals views reality from the opposite end of the telescope from the New Left. Hook's reputation as one of the major American intellects of this century is secure. Feuer is a respected and successful academic who has published widely. They are comfortable men who travel among the famous and the affluent. They see little pain or suffering, since, as Michael Harrington pointed out, the Other Americans are invisible men. What they do see, however, is their own tragic affair with Communism, and they are determined the new generation should not whore after the same bitch.

On the other hand, the New Radicals have made it an article of faith to see the world with the eyes of the excluded, to empathize with them totally, and to speak with them against leaders and elites. SNCC's Stokely Carmichael says, "The basic difference between us and the liberals comes from what you see when you get up in the morning. We see sharecroppers and they see Central Park." And Casey Hayden, writing in *The New Republic*, commented, "My work has been with the poor. The main thing I've learned is to see the world from their perspective: from the bottom."

Given their opposite perspectives, the ex-radicals and the New Radicals are logical polarities. Lacking the pain and poverty of the excluded, the ex-radicals would probably agree with Seymour Martin Lipset's opinion that "Democracy is not only, or even primarily, a means through which different groups can attain their ends or seek the good society; it is the good society itself in operation." The New Radicals, correctly, I think, would deny that America, because it has the formal institutions of democracy, is "the good society itself in operation." Therefore, they call for a "radical reconstruction" of that society, while the Panglossian ex-radicals celebrate the status quo and trumpet the end of ideology.

The ex-radicals have also segregated ethics from politics, while one of the cardinal tenets of the New Left is that morality and politics are indivisible. Daniel Bell has written that ethics is concerned with justice, while concrete politics involves "a power struggle between organized groups to determine the allocation of privilege." Or as Lyndon Johnson and others have phrased it, "Politics is the art of the possible." The New Left insists politics become the art of the impossible. It agrees with Max Weber, who wrote, "Certainly all historical experience confirms the truth that man would not have attained the possible unless time and again he had reached out for the impossible." That is the idea implicit in Carl Oglesby's statement that the goal of the New Left is to make love more possible.

The New Left and the important school of social critics including not just Hook and Feuer, but Irving Kristol, Seymour Lipset, Max Lerner, and John Roche, perceive Communism from a vantage point separated by two decades. The ex-radicals see Communism as it was in the 1930's: ruthless, Messianic, totalitarian, conspiratorial, monolithic, militaristic, genocidal. The purges, the Hitler-Stalin pact, the Soviet invasion of Finland, are still haunting obscenities to these men. So obsessive is their anti-Communism that Hook, during the 1950's, opposed repeal of the Smith Act.

But the New Left sees Communism quite differently. If a New Left activist is now twenty-two, he doesn't remember the Soviet Union's absorption of a satellite empire in the 1940's or the crushing of the Hungarian revolt in 1956. But he does remember that in April of 1961 America gave covert support to the Bay of Pigs invasion. He does remember America's increasing involvement in Vietnam and the indefensible intervention in the Dominican Republic in April of 1965. During the same period of time, this mythical twenty-two-year-old New Radical has seen the Soviet Union remove its missiles from Cuba, sign the nuclear test-ban treaty, intervene in the internal affairs of no other nation, and play peacemaker between India and Pakistan. Also, he has seen anti-Communism wed only to racism, militarism, and reaction in America. He cannot conceptualize a progressive anti-Communism, only the anti-Communism of those who oppose SNCC, SDS, the FSM, and the anti-war movements. He has seen Communists only as victims, never as executioners. He has seen Communists denied burial in Arlington Cemetery, pilloried before HUAC, denied free speech on the campuses.

The FSM at Berkeley crystallized almost all the differences between the 1930's ex-radicals and the New Left. The FSM was anti-status quo, valued ethics above law and order, had its own hip-anarchic style, and included everyone from Maoists to Goldwaterites. So although the Berkeley faculty voted 8 to 1 to support the students against the administration, the most vehement attacks on the FSM came from the typewriters of Dr. Hook and Professors Feuer, Lipsit, and Nathan Glazer, in publications like *The New Leader*, *Commentary*, and *The Reporter*.

Professor Feuer's *New Leader* essay was extraordinary for its

ceived 1 million votes for President. In 1932, with a much larger electorate and millions unemployed, Norman Thomas also received 1 million votes. During the 1930's the Socialists helped in building important unions like the ILGWU, the Textile Workers, and the UAW.

Since 1960, however, the Socialist Party has just been a holding company for an ideal. The party's membership has dwindled to a few thousand members, mostly elderly people, who are fragmented into a rainbow of sectarian factions. The party's youth affiliate, the Young People's Socialist League, was suspended in 1964 for ultra-Leftism, and is now virtually a paper organization. The largest Socialist publication, *Dissent*, has a circulation of about 5,000. The League for Industrial Democracy is just beginning to be revivified after a long period of inactivity.

Still, this tradition has produced a remarkable group of intellectuals, among them Irving Howe, the forty-five-year-old editor of *Dissent*, and fifty-three-year-old civil-rights tactician and theorist, Bayard Rustin. Both men are anti-Communist radicals. They oppose the war in Vietnam, condemned U.S. intervention in the Dominican Republic, and have socialist economic goals. They advocate the necessity of civil disobedience and supported the FSM. Howe particularly has often clashed publicly with ex-radicals like Hook and Professor Roche.

But there are sharp differences between the Social Democrats and the New Left. One of them is emotional. The Social Democrats belong to a clearly defined historical tradition they are proud of. The New Left sees the Socialists merely as part of the "whole rotten bag" called the Old Left, and therefore as similar to their instinctive enemies the Stalinists and the Trotskyites. The Socialists believe that what divides them from the other Old Left sects is the essence of political morality. The New Left sees the whole Old Left implicated in the legacy of factionalism and failure.

Another difference is one of style. Howe and Rustin are cocky intellectuals who relish debate and hairsplitting. The New Left prefers communitarian consensus to give-and-take debate, fearing such debate inevitably leads to that fatal Old Left disease called factionalism. So the New Left, by choice, remains communal and vague, and the Social Democrats jab at its inconsistencies like skilled but insensitive matadors.

Finally, there are two authentic political disagreements, each clarified and intensified by a specific event. One is the question of agency of social change. The older Socialists, chastened by failure, believe in a reformist coalition of the labor movement, the major civil-rights groups, the churches, the liberals, and the intellectuals reforming the Democratic Party. The visionary New Radicals believe in creating independent and insurgent constituencies outside—sometimes against—Establishment institutions. Irving Howe calls the New Left's strategy "go-it-aloneism," and Rustin calls it romanticism and infantile purity. The New Left, on the other hand, points out that the poor have no say in the decision-making in these national liberal groupings, that the labor movement is hopelessly bureaucratized and, on issues like foreign policy and civil rights, more conservative than both the Government and the Church.

The Socialists and the New Left also disagree about Communism. The disagreement is not so wide or so unbridgeable as it is with the ex-radicals; it is tactical and emotional rather than philosophical. The difference resolves mostly around the issue of exclusion of Communists from organizations and political alliances. The Socialists, unlike some of the ex-radicals, defend every civil liberty of the Communists. But they argue that no mass-based American movement can be built that is compromised by Communism, and therefore Communists should be excluded, although allowed to form their own organizations. The New Left argues that Communists are not a special breed of dissenter, that a movement fighting for freedom for one group cannot at the same time deny freedom to another group, and that the dangers of cooperating with George Meany are greater than permitting an eighteen-year-old Communist into its own democratic organizations.

The coalition-versus-insurgent organizing issue was crystallized at the 1964 Democratic national convention. To honky-tonk Atlantic City came the anti-Establishment Mississippi Freedom Democratic Party: sixty-four poor rural Negroes and four white integrationists. Their only credentials, as Murray Kempton wrote, were "their wounds and their faces." They came to challenge the right of the regular segregationist delegation to represent Mississippi at the convention. The MFDP said they represented the 850,000 unregistered Negroes of the Magnolia State.

At first it seemed as if the poor petitioners' challenge would be brushed aside as a rude intrusion on Lyndon Johnson's ceremonial coronation. But forty-eight hours before the convention opened, the credentials committee held a nationally televised hearing that shamed the nation's conscience, already in mourning for the murders of Andrew Goodman, James Chaney, and Michael Schwerner.

Joseph Rauh, former leader of the ADA and the MFDP lawyer, told the committee, "I have only an hour to tell you a story of moral agony that could take years."

Edward King, the oft-beaten white minister at Tougaloo College, said, "We do not apologize for not holding our convention in Neshoba County."

Martin Luther King, Roy Wilkins, and James Farmer all testified for the Freedom Democrats. Before the day was out liberal Democrats like Congresswoman Edith Green and Senator Wayne Morse had been won to the MFDP's side. The rude intrusion suddenly became a specter threatening to tear the Democratic Party open.

The intrigues of the next seventy-two hours are lost in the half truths of sleepless men. While thousands of students and civil-rights workers kept vigil on the boardwalk, intricate negotiations were undertaken by Rauh, Hubert Humphrey (whose own vice presidential hopes were in the balance), and the national civil-rights leadership. By Tuesday morning the President offered the MFDP two seats at-large plus a guarantee that all future convention delegations would be integrated.

There followed a dramatic caucus in a Negro church, where Roy Wilkens, Walter Reuther, Wayne Morse, Martin Luther King, and Bayard Rustin came to urge the delegation of cotton-choppers and maids to accept the two-seat compromise as an "incredible triumph." James Farmer took an agnostic position, while James Forman and Bob Parris of SNCC urged rejection of the "back-of-the-bus" compromise. The delegates finally voted unanimously to reject the compromise.

The liberals, civil-rights leaders, and Social Democrats were shocked. One of them said, "Those fools snatched defeat from the jaws of victory." They suddenly realized the New Radicals were uncompromising Utopians who would not abide by all the rules of polite protest. They realized there was *revolutionary feeling* within the movement, and that the anti-leader anarchism was real and ran deep.

For their part, SNCC and the MFDP discovered their liberal friends cared more about the threat of Goldwater and the ambitions of Humphrey than about the absolute morality of a cause; they discovered that even the best liberals, those who sometimes supported civil disobedience, would at some point divide politics and morality and bend their knees to reality.

In the months that followed, Atlantic City became an irrational watershed—or Krondtadt—for both the Social Democrats and the New Left. People who had not been there, like Irving Howe and Nat Hentoff, chose up sides. No one seemed to disagree with his political allies who had been there. The decision against the compromise became a metaphor whereby everyone defined the emotional intensity of his radicalism. Those who opposed the compromise were branded irrational, destructive, and nihilistic.

Those who supported it were labeled sell-outs, lackies of the President, betrayers of the radical creed. The Socialists decided the students needed a political education about how to function in the grown-up world of *realpolitik*, and the students decided the Social Democrats' coalition would always turn on the poor as it had in Atlantic City.

All of this was unnecessary and tragic. There were good people on both sides of the dispute; there seems to be no right and wrong position, no great principle involved. Certainly the great principle the New Left claims was at stake—decision-making by the poor— is a myth. The SNCC workers almost handpicked the MFDP delegation in Mississippi, and controlled it while at the convention.

The unreal and unnecessary nature of the Atlantic City debate, I think, extends to most of the furor over coalition politics as opposed to what SDS calls "the creation of popular left opposition." Both are needed.

The Social Democratic Left is composed of an infinitesimal number of radical intellectuals. Their task is to criticize and radicalize adult liberal and Government institutions, and not to coach the New Left. The New Radicals, meanwhile, are right to organize independently of the mainstream institutions, although I think they romanticize the radical potential of the underclass, and underestimate the radical potential among the alienated white-collar sections of the middle class, like teachers and welfare workers. Except for rare head-on confrontations such as the one in Atlantic City, there need not be prolonged, often slanderous polemics about these alternate, but not contradictory, theories about the agency of social change. Irving Howe cannot quit his teaching and writing jobs to join the SDS Community Union in Newark, and Tom Hayden cannot abandon his organizing work to become an adviser to Walter Reuther. Each has his own function. The Socialists have no coalition and the New Left has only small movement. Let each one build his own bridge across the Generation Gap rather than tear the other's down.

On April 17, 1965, SDS sponsored a national protest in Washington against the war in Vietnam. Speakers at the rally included I. F. Stone, Senator Ernest Gruening, Staughton Lynd, Bob Parris, and Paul Potter. As sole sponsor, SDS agreed that anyone might participate in the march, regardless of political belief, including previously excluded pariahs like Chinese- and Soviet-style Communists.

As the date of the march drew closer, several adult peace leaders began to fear that the protest had been taken over by extremist or anti-American elements. In San Francisco, Robert Pickus, the Western regional director of Turn Towards Peace (TTP), distributed a press release disassociating TTP from the protest, stating, "It is time that someone within the peace movement challenged activity which is in fact more hostile to America than to war."

In the East, Robert Gilmore, the executive director of TTP, privately sought to persuade several national peace leaders to detach themselves from the SDS march because it had accepted the endorsement of the W. E. B. Du Bois Clubs and the May 2nd Movement. Gilmore argued that the "tone" of the speeches would be anti-American and that the possibility of massive civil disobedience existed. Finally, on the eve of the march, a memo was released by eleven adult peace leaders that was a clear attack on the SDS protest. The statement was signed by Norman Thomas, Bayard Rustin, H. Stuart Hughes, Robert Gilmore, A. J. Muste, and seven others. While praising the spirit of the demonstration, the memo also asserted:

> We join in the concern about developments in Vietnam, even though we disagree with particular positions expressed by some elements of the March. . . .
>
> In the effort to register such concerns with our govern-

ment and people, we welcome the cooperation of all those groups and individuals who, like ourselves, believe in the need for an independent peace movement, not committed to any form of totalitarianism nor drawing inspiration or direction from the foreign policy of any government.

That is an unexceptional statement. But when it was released twelve hours before the SDS march, the students rightly felt they were being red-baited in a crude code language. On the day of the march, the *New York Post* published an editorial quoting from the memo and observing:

> several leaders of the peace movement have taken clear note of attempts to convert the event into a pro-Communist production. . . . there is no justification for transforming the march into a frenzied, one-sided anti-American show.

The march itself vindicated SDS, and later several of the memo's signatories, including H. Stuart Hughes and A. J. Muste, apologized for signing it. Instead of being the "frenzied, one-sided anti-American show," the *Post* feared, the march proved to be the setting for an exceptionally moving, humanistic appeal by Stone, who said:

"The men directing America's cruel policies are decent human beings like you and me, who are caught up in monstrous institutions that have a life of their own." He urged the 20,000 demonstrators to "go home and talk about these things, but not in tones of hatred and self-righteousness. We have to get out of this reign of hatred."

Later Stone addressed

> previous generations of snotty Marxist-Leninists who looked down on us liberals [and] became reactionaries, and some of them FBI agents. . . . When you consider the pressures for conformity in Washington today, and especially within the

President's own party, and look at Senator Gruening today, we liberals haven't done so badly.

The bitter debates generated by the memo served to polarize the groupings on each side of the question of exclusion of Communists. The over-thirty liberal and Social Democratic organizations—SANE, the ADA, the LID, the ACLU—do try to exclude from membership individuals they consider to be Communists. The movements of the New Left—SNCC, SDS, the VDC, SSOC —do not exclude *anyone*.

I think it is in this area that the New Radicals have much to teach the old. Before the death of Stalin in 1953, a hard organizational line against Communists appeared to have made sense. They were, after all, a disciplined, anti-democratic, monolithic movement that had traditionally subverted liberal and single-issue organizations for ends that served Moscow. Howe was right to be an exclusionist ten years ago.

But not only does Communism come in 57 varieties today, its relation to student groups is very different than was its relationship to adult cultural, labor, or anti-fascist groups in the 1930's. First, the New Radicalism is a reaction to the failure of the old. And one of the reasons the old failed was that it was torn asunder by Communist-anti-Communist fratricides. The New Radicals reject both fanatic religions. They know how the "old fights" were prosecuted by both sides *without regard for human feelings.*

Second, the student groups today are too decentralized and anti-ideological to be captured by any manipulative cadre. This is a statement that may sound naïve to those unfamiliar with the inner life of the movement. It can't be proved, but I am confident it is so. The New Radicals may not be "turned off" by Communist politics, but they are "turned off" by Communist style—the style of the cautious, elitist, Puritanical, rigid, mechanical bureaucrat. Virtually with his last breath Prince Kropotkin denounced Lenin, and so it is within the student groupings: the anarchist spirit will not be tamed by either official liberalism or bureaucratic collectivism.

Third is the fact that the New Radicals are still kids, many of them seventeen or twenty years old. Their politics are not a finished product. Most of them haven't yet read the writers who will define their values more clearly. They are open and searching. Even those emotionally *simpatico* with the Chinese or Cuban revolutions are not moral monsters. They are not comparable to the hard, ruthless party aparatchiks of the 1930's. They should be exposed to the democratic atmosphere of SDS, not sealed off hermetically into an Outer Darkness where they will be forced to subsist on the half facts of the *National Guardian* and PL. Why do Social Democrats always fear that political influence inevitably flows one way, and that it is the democrats who must get subverted? Do bad ideas necessarily drive out good ideas?

I think the possibility of salvation exists even among some alienated youth on the right. I recently covered a Young Americans for Freedom rally in Manhattan, and found the YAF types sharing many assumptions with the New Radicals. They spoke out against the hypocritical cant of liberal politicians, against impersonal oligarchies that encroached on their individual freedom; they fretted about drab vocational opportunities, and felt, in general, betrayed by the adult world. They talked about Barry Goldwater the way SDSers talk about Hubert Humphrey. They, like the youngsters Irving Howe would quarantine, are part of the same ambience and mood. When I asked a YAF high school girl why she was a conservative, she said, "Because I don't want to be either a victim or an executioner." That she probably meant a "victim" of Asiatic Communism or a Negro rapist should not be ignored. But neither should the fact that she quoted an existential radical who counseled that rebellion itself was a valid protest against an absurd world.

Lastly, what is the actual process by which Communists are to be excluded? Do you do it with loyalty oaths and purges, the very tools of McCarthyism that have made the New Radicals see the Communists only as "the enemy of my enemy"? Do you do it by inserting ritualistic slogans about totalitarianism into constitutions, which only infuriate anti-Cold War liberals? How do you even tell who is, and who isn't, a Communist?

Exclusionism denies three of the root ideals of the New Radicalism. That human freedom and participation should be extended. That every individual is noble. That a new society based on love and trust must be created.

Memos like the one signed by Rustin, Gilmore, and the others create Communists, just as Senator Fulbright pointed out that America's Dominican intervention created thousands of *Fidelistas* throughout Latin America. Such memos isolate the Social Democrats, not those they think are Communists.

A small group of intellectuals and journalists have clustered themselves around the emerging Left and made it their base. They have seized upon the fuzziest currents in the New Radicalism and have fashioned them into a countercatechism to match the dogmatism of the Social Democrats. This grouping, which is led by Yale professor Staughton Lynd, has taken the movement's romanticism, its blurring of Camus' "tragic dividing line" between violence and nonviolence, and its abusive generational solidarity, and made of these aberrations a political tendency.

This Romantic Left grouping has a large following inside the new movements. Especially does the charismatic thirty-six-year-old Lynd, whom *The New York Times Magazine* correctly termed "elder statesman and doyen theoretician of the New Left." My fear is that the effect of this grouping will be to harden the generational lines, and thereby diminish the chances for the forging of a broadly based opposition movement to the Johnson consensus. Just as the Social Democrats excommunicate anyone from their church who supports the heretic Cuban revolution, the Romantic Left is equally fanatical in purging those "ex-radicals" who choose to work within, or alongside of, the "devilish" Establishment. Neither church, I suspect, is ecumenical enough.

Lynd, whose politics sometimes seem a tortured mixture of Thoreau and John Brown, has the temperament of an archetypal romantic revolutionary. Mutual friends have told me touching stories illustrating Lynd's sensitive instincts; according to one, he quit the Fieldston High School football team when he felt sorry for classmates who would have no athletic letter to gloat over. Lynd's bearing is open, earnest, gentle. Once, during a debate, TTP's Robert Pickus alluded to "Mr. Lynd's sneaky Quaker manner."

The son of Robert and Helen Lynd, authors of the celebrated *Middletown* sociological study, Lynd attended Ethical Culture private schools. At Harvard he joined the John Reed Club, and was a national youth leader in the Henry Wallace campaign of 1948. The next year he had a brief and uncharacteristic flirtation with Trotskyism. But he quickly bounced back to his more emotional and mystical brand of radicalism, and in 1953 registered as a conscientious objector. Starting in 1954, he spent three idyllic years at the Macedonia Cooperative Community in northeast Georgia, where the Brook Farm atmosphere harmonized with Lynd's transcendentalist spirit.

From there, Lynd's life took on a searching, experimental quality similar to that of Forman, Parris, and Oglesby, those over-thirty radicals who had to wait for the post-sit-in generation to end their odyssey. Lynd spent a brief period at another cooperative community in New Jersey, and then moved on to become a community organizer for the Union Settlement House on Manhattan's Lower East Side. While there, he published several critiques of bulldozer urban renewal in the vein that Jane Jacobs was to popularize a few years later.

Between 1961 and 1964 Lynd taught history at Spelman College, a Negro women's school in Atlanta. It was there that his complex radicalism gained an additional strand from his deep involvement with SNCC. In the summer of 1964 Lynd was director of the freedom schools division of the Mississippi Summer Project, and at the end of the summer he accepted a teaching post at Yale University.

In 1965 his radicalism, already a mix of Quaker pacifism, orthodox Marxism, romantic transcendentalism, and SNCC Populism, took on a symbolic dimension as well. First Lynd refused to pay three hundred dollars on his federal income tax, in protest against the war in Vietnam. Then he helped organize the Assembly of Unrepresented People in Washington, which symbolically declared peace directly with "the people of Vietnam," circumventing all governments. And then, in 1966, as soon as the W. E. B. Du Bois Clubs were attacked as a "communist front group" by the Attorney General, Lynd announced that he was joining the organization in a symbolic act of solidarity. Such pure, heroic gestures make Lynd the closest thing the New Left has to a *Zeitgeist*.

Reading through Lynd's output of essays, one is appalled that a scholar wrote them—they are so bereft of systematic thought, and so full of suggestions for cathartic fantasies. The purity of Lynd's moral anguish shimmers behind every phrase, but the politics are otherworldly, more in the spirit of LSD than SDS. In *Liberation* Lynd wrote:

"We have moved into a twilight zone between democratically delegated authority and something actually called 'fascism.' "

In the same article, describing the SDS March on Washington, he says:

> Still more poignant was the perception . . . that as the crowd moved down the mall toward the seat of government, its path delimited on each side by rows of chartered buses so that there was nowhere else to go but forward, toward the waiting policemen, it seemed that the great mass of people would simply flow on through and over the marble buildings, that our forward movement was irresistibly strong, that

had some been shot or arrested nothing could have stopped that crowd from taking possession of its Government. Perhaps next time we should keep going. . . .

I was part of that "great mass of people" and empathize with Lynd's romantic feeling. But what right do 20,000 people have, even symbolically, to take possession of their Government when it is clear that a majority of their fellow citizens support the Vietnam policy of that Government? For 20,000 people, representing at best the opinion of one-fifth of the country, to take power is not a very solid basis for democracy. And to seriously propose such a strategy for the anti-war movement is to invite violent repression, bloodshed, and an abortion of the New Left.

In his wildly applauded speech at the mass teach-in at Berkeley, in May of 1965, Lynd attacked the Social Democrats' coalition theory as "coalition with the marines" because of the war in Vietnam. He then gave his vision of an alternate strategy:

I am advocating non-violent retirement of the present Administration, that is, the creation of civil disobedience so persistent and so massive that the Tuesday lunch club which runs this country—Johnson, Rusk, McNamara, Bundy—will forthwith resign. . . . we cannot wait until the next presidential election in 1968. Therefore we must vote with our feet by marching and picketing; if necessary vote with our backsides by sitting in jail. . . . In the 1840's Thoreau said that one man ready to die could stop slavery in America. I think all of us here this week-end should search our hearts for the courage and clarity of spirit to go to the White House, go to the Oakland Army Terminal, if possible go to Vietnam and stand in front of the flamethrowers, and say: "If blood must be spilt, let it be mine, and stop killing Vietnamese children. If you must search and destroy, let me save you the trouble, here I am."

The young man who gave up his high-school letter out of sympathy for his less athletic classmates can understandably utter such despairing words when he sees his country commit mass murder in Vietnam. But such noble emotions are not the basis for effective politics; purgative politics, maybe; religious politics, maybe; but not politics that can mobilize new constituencies and make the Government change its policy.

Another example of Lynd's absolutist emotionalism came in an article he co-authored with Tom Hayden in *Studies on the Left*. They wrote:

> . . . we refuse to be anti-communist. We insist that the term has lost all the specific content it once had. Instead it serves as the key category of abstract thought which Americans use to justify a foreign policy that often is no more sophisticated than rape. . . .

Communism is polycentric. Communism in East Germany is different from its Polish variant. Authentic democrats like I. F. Stone can, in good conscience, support the Cuban revolution. But still, anti-Communism hasn't lost "*all* the specific content it once had." Keynesian economics, corporate planning, and welfare reforms haven't made it irrelevant to be anti-capitalist. Communism still stands for a social system without the essentials of formal democracy—a free press, opposition parties, or an independent judiciary. That is something worth being against for moral and political reasons. I would not give anti-Communism the priority the ex-radicals and the Social Democrats do, and I am opposed to their exclusionist position. But I am still for being anti-Communist as one way of affirming one's positive belief in democracy, as a way of saying Milovan Djilas should not be imprisoned, and that there should be freedom of speech, religion, and assembly in the Soviet Union.

The last of Lynd's positions that I think the New Left should question is his assertion that there is nothing wrong with the National Liberation Front's use of violence and terror, and that American pacifists have no right to recommend nonviolent tactics to the Vietcong.

Camus wrote there was a "tragic dividing line" between "those who accept the consequences of being murderers themselves or the accomplices of murderers, and those who refuse to do so with all their force and being." And in his statement on the Algerian revolution Camus wrote, "To justify himself, each relies on the other's crimes. But that is a casuistry of the blood. . . ."

Now I know that Lynd and the rest of the Romantic Left personally wouldn't swat a fly. Yet they blur Camus' "tragic dividing line" when they romanticize violence in Vietnam and elsewhere. Carl Oglesby, who says he wants to create a world in which love is more possible, can approvingly tell the November, 1965, SANE peace march, "Revolutions do not take place in velvet boxes. . . . Nuns will be raped and bureaucrats will be disemboweled. . . ."

I think the Romantic Left and the ex-radicals make the opposite mistake. The ex-radicals say that America is almost perfect and that politics is just the juggling of interest groups. The Romantic Left says that America is on the verge of fascism and that anything goes in the effort to change it.

Max Weber cited three qualities a great political leader must have: "passion," "a feeling of responsibility," and "a sense of proportion." The ex-radicals lack the first quality and have an excess of the other two. The Romantic Left has only the first. If it had the last two it would not sanction the disemboweling of bureaucrats.

Since the New Left is essentially traditionless itself, it is appropriate that the movement's most prolific popularizer should be such a basically unpolitical man as Nat Hentoff. Hentoff is an informed jazz critic, a sharp-eyed observer of the managed press, and one of *The New Yorker's* most fluent house writers. But grinding out computerized material for such varied outlets as *Status*, *Playboy*, *Liberation* and *The Partisan Review*, Hentoff is far removed from both the internal life of the New Left and the realities of power in Washington. Thus, Hentoff's ultra-revolutionary rhetoric resounds like a pop-art echo in a vacuum. Someone like Norman Mailer is, in his personal life, equally distant from the movement and the founts of power, but his intuitive and existential insights are so true that he commands our respect. But Hentoff's magpie snatchings from other writers are merely prescriptions for revolutionary purity and political irrelevance.

In the February, 1966, issue of *Evergreen Review*, Hentoff informed the underground that the Northern Student Movement had "2,000 members on 73 campuses" and that SNCC had "200 paid workers and 250 full-time volunteers." The fact is that the NSM has zero members on zero campuses because it doesn't believe in campus chapters. Executive secretary William Strickland defines NSM's function as "organizing other organizers." SNCC, as of January, 1966, had less than 120 paid workers; only during summer vacations do its volunteers ever approach the 250 number.

In his voluminous writings Hentoff adopts a narrow, sectarian stance toward the New Left. He defines it to include only activist members of national organizations, ignoring the thousands of less militant young people who show up for demonstrations and reluctantly pursue career goals. Hentoff insists anyone cooperating with Establishment organizations or disputing any canon of the New Left—for example, anyone supporting the Atlantic City compromise—is an "ex-radical." He hurled that epithet at Rustin less than year after he had dedicated his book, *The New Equality*, to Rustin. By Hentoff's purist standards, then, Martin Luther King and Michael Harrington would also be liberals and not to be trusted as allies.

Hentoff's strategy for social change is a purist alliance of the poor and the students, both remaining uncontaminated by such corrupting agencies of change as the Democratic Party, the SCLC, and SANE. But the unpolitical Hentoff romanticizes the poor no less than the most naïve SDS recruit. He forgets that there is nothing inherently radical (or virtuous) about the poor. He forgets the poor are the most anti-Communist class in America; were the major constituency of Fascism in Germany and Italy and of Peronism in Argentina; and are only 20 perecent of the population.

Before the sit-in movement began Hentoff exhibited little interest in politics, and like the latest convert to any cause, he displays the greatest fanatical fervor; so much so that he can excommunicate someone like Rustin, who suffered for his pacifist principles in jail during World War II. Thus, true-believer Hentoff can counsel the New Radicals in a *Liberation* article not to "waste much of their time in 'dialogues' with their elders."

I can't think of a more destructive piece of advice to give the New Left. Part of the contribution of the new movements has been to breathe new life into the older liberal groups like SANE, the ACLU, and the churches. SANE would never have thought of marching on Washington if SDS hadn't proved it could be done seven months before. Organizations like the ACLU and SANE are just now beginning to reconsider their own exclusionist policies after watching and debating with the New Left. To argue that the New Radicals have *nothing* to learn from "their elders" is to deny the value of all existing wisdom and guarantee that the New Left will end up an exotic Union Square splinter like the De Leonists and the Cannonites. The goal of radicalism is to improve the human condition, not to prove one's own moral superiority.

Growing up outside of all existing radical traditions, and having no ready-made adult organization to graduate into, is a nagging problem confronting the New Radicals. There is, however, a broad, amorphous political tradition I think they can be enriched by. It is the humanist liberal tradition represented by Jefferson, John Stuart Mill, John Dewey, Albert Camus, George Orwell, and Martin Luther King. This is the tradition I suspect Max Weber had in the back of his mind when he urged the fusion of "the ethic of responsibility" with the "ethic of absolute ends." As always, there are not many parishioners at this ecumenical church today, although Arthur Waskow and I. F. Stone are among them. Nevertheless, it is my feeling that the point at which the ideas and values of Stone and Waskow overlap with those of SDS is the point from which a democratic Left opposition against the Great Society can grow.

The Humanist Liberals are not ideological or factional purists. They synthesize visionary, communal ends with a sobering realism about how you win power in this pluralistic, technocratic society of almost 200 million. They understand the enormity of the state power they are challenging; it is not coincidental that Stone and Waskow are stationed in Washington, while Lynd is in New Haven. Although not necessarily socialists, the Humanist Liberals are comfortable with people to their left. Not having a traumatic tradition to defend like the Social Democrats, they are less emotional in their anti-Communism and less beguiled by the labor metaphysic Mills so vehemently argued against late in his life. On the issue of anti-Communism Waskow said in *Dissent* of the New Radicals:

". . . they have learned a great deal about the corruptiveness of Stalinist technique—but what they have learned is that they should not act like Stalinists, not that the Stalinists should be purged."

It seems that one of the most progressive effects of the New Left has been on liberal groupings midway between the insurgent movements themselves and the Establishment. In this limbo I would put organizations like SANE and the LID, Senators like Morse and Robert Kennedy, institutions like the Institute for Policy Studies (IPS), and publications like *The New Republic* and *The Village Voice*.

A textbook example of this gradual liberating process has been the National Student Association, which a few years ago voted down SDS national secretary Paul Booth as International Affairs Vice President and refused to endorse civil disobedience. At its 1965 congress, NSA adopted resolutions that:

Urged immediate cessation of all offensive military action in Vietnam.

Proposed admission of Communist China to the United Nations and condemned U.S. intervention in the Dominican Republic.

Proposed the establishment of a federal police force to protect civil-rights activists.

Endorsed nonviolent rent strikes, boycotts, and other forms of civil disobedience, in a reversal of its earlier policy.

And when the congress ended, the three hundred students—mostly campus politicos and not movement militants—spontaneously linked arms and sang the New Left's anthem: "We Shall Overcome."

The Humanist Liberals understand what the Romantic Left does not—that NSA-type liberals and the moderate, middle-class readers of *The New Republic* are allies, not enemies, and should be an integral part of any new constituencies, or of any new politics that is to be rooted in moral values. While the Romantic Left manufactures the equivalent of litmus tests to prove absolute purity, two of SDS's most talented members, Paul Booth and Lee Webb, have published a paper that says:

"We are not opposed to the new motion in the churches, in some unions, even in some agencies of government like the Peace Corps. In fact, we welcome it. . . . We are not satisfied with a facile anti-establishment position which suggests that the Peace Corps and the Air Force are equally the enemy."

What is required, then, to bridge the Generation Gap is what Waskow proposed in *Dissent*—"a meta-coalition between 'the movement' and 'the coalition' . . . with knowledgeable and sympathetic 'politicotherapists' helping translate between the two sides and suggest where each can move forward in its own way without trampling the other."

The first concrete step toward this coalition between the Humanist Liberals and the New Radicals came early in 1966 with the formation of the National Conference for the New Politics, with Waskow, and Paul Albert of Californians for Liberal Representation, acting as organizational midwives and SNCC's Julian Bond and the CDC's Si Cassidy its co-chairmen.

This loose, well-financed, electoral-oriented, nonmembership alliance includes SNCC; SDS; the MFDP; local radical insurgents like the grape strikers in California, and *ad hoc* anti-war committees; SANE, the academic leaders of the teach-in movement; unions like the Teamsters and some old CIO locals; grass-roots Democratic Party reformers from New York, Texas, Illinois, California, and Michigan; and intellectuals like Eric Fromm, Nat Hentoff, H. Stuart Hughes and Dr. Harold Taylor.

The New Radicals are speaking harsh truths in a new and irreverent voice. They are saying that Communism is changing, and that positions frozen a decade ago must be reconsidered. They are saying that the whole society—from the academy to the anti-poverty program—has become too bureaucratized and must be decentralized and humanized. They are saying the draft is undemocratic. They are saying that revolutions are tearing the colonial clamps off three continents, and that America must stand with the poor and not the powerful. They are saying that automation is making a guaranteed annual income and a redefinition of work imperative. They are saying that ethics and politics have become divided and must be reunited.

If they are emotional or badly informed about other things, on all these issues the New Radicals are right. The older dissenters should pause and acknowledge these new voices before the Generation Gap becomes a canyon of mistrust.

Chapter 9
The Future

Oh, deep in my heart, I do believe we shall overcome, someday.
—FREEDOM SONG

Give flowers to the rebels failed.
—ANARCHIST POEM

■ A prophetic minority creates each generation's legend. In the 1920's it was the expatriate quest for personal expression. In the 1930's it was radical social action. In the 1940's it was the heroism of the trenches. In the 1950's it was the cultivation of the private self. Now, halfway through the decade, it is once again the ideal of social action that is *defining a generation.*

By this I mean specifically that in fifteen years Bob Dylan's poems will be taught in college classrooms, that Paul Booth, Julian Bond, and Stokely Carmichael will be the leaders of adult protest movements, that the Beatles movies will be revived in art houses, and that Tom Hayden, Norman Fruchter, Robb Burlage, Bob Parris, and Carl Oglesby will be major social critics. But I also mean to emphasize that the New Left has, and always will have, only a fraction of the whole truth, just as the Freudians, the Symbolists, Marxists and the Impressionists possessed only a fragment of the truth. But it is the fragment glimpsed by this generation.

The legend of the 1930's turned to ashes in Washington, Moscow, and Madrid before the decade was over. It is entirely possible that the New Left can meet such a tragic end as well. The possibility of political fissures exists in any movement. This one could split over tactics like the Bolsheviks or Mensheviks, or over morality like Sartre and Camus. Black nationalism may yet poison it, and unfocused activism may exhaust it. But I doubt it.

In the immediate future, the impulse to rebel will continue to grow among marginal groups like students, Negroes, migrant farm workers, intellectuals, and white-collar workers. This will happen because the generators of dissent—war, bureaucracy, guilt-producing affluence, racism, hypocrisy, moral rot—are enduring in the fabric of American society. If the Vietnam war is settled, there will be another one in Thailand, or Angola, or Peru. If Bobby Baker is jailed, there will be another fast buck politician exposed. If the killers of Goodman, Chaney, and Schwerner are convicted, there will be other atrocities in the South.

All this means that the New Left—and the other sections of the society in motion—will grow and become even more uncomfortably radical. My own hunch is that SDS will be the chief repository of this radical mood, that SNCC's time has passed, its gifts taken without adequate acknowledgment. I also suspect the Hereditary Left will not grow much, because it is too weighted down with the moral bankruptcy of Communism, and because it misses completely this generation's indictment of impersonal bureaucracies and the existential void of the middle class. Primarily, the New Left will become increasingly the umbrella under which indigenous, decentralized movements will grow. Grass-roots insurgencies, such as the grape strike in California, Berkeley's Vietnam Day Committee, the NCUP project in Newark, the Lowndes County Freedom Organization in Alabama, Dick Gregory's campaign for mayor of Chicago, independent community committees against the war in Vietnam, and campus protests against the draft like those at Chicago and CCNY, are the shadows of the future. National organizations are not the style of anarchists and improvisers.

Beneath this nation's gleaming surface of computers, Hilton hotels, and super-highways, there are latent volcanoes of violence. These volcanoes have erupted tragically in Birmingham, Mississippi, and Dallas in 1963; in Harlem and Rochester in 1964; in Watts and Selma in 1965; and in Watts and in Mississippi again in 1966. Riot and assassination are symptoms of the disease in our society below the Disneyland façade. The New Radicals will rub these hidden sores until they bleed, or until the Great Society begins to heal the one in five who are poor, and the millions who are voteless, powerless, victimized, and mad.

But two yawning pitfalls stretch out before the New Left, diluting the chances of its growth. One is the rising tide of domestic McCarthyism, which is paralleling the escalation of the war in Vietnam. The other is the culture's spongelike genius for either absorbing or merchandizing all dissent.

If the Great Society becomes preoccupied by a narrow choice between "guns and butter," then it will become impossible even to hold up the alternate vision of "bread and roses." Already some social welfare and anti-poverty programs are not being funded, and New York's reform Congressman, William F. Ryan, has quipped, "Johnson is asking us to choose between guns and oleo."

There has always been a latent anti-intellectual strain to the American character, as Richard Hofstadter documented in his Pulitzer Prize-winning book, *Anti-intellectualism in American Life*. The country's repudiation of Adlai Stevenson and the upsurge of McCarthyism in the 1950's were the latest expression of attitudes that go back to the Alien and Sedition Acts and the Salem witch trials. Now, as the Vietnam war grows more bloody, the stalemate more frustrating, there seems to be a resurgence of paranoid know-nothing sentiment throughout the country. My fear is that if the war drags on, and there are 400,000 American troops in Vietnam at the start of 1967, then all of America will begin to close down, just as the nation turned in on itself during the Korean war, or as France became repressive during the last stages of its seven-year conflict with Algeria. If this happens, then all bets are off on the future of the New Left. Its elite will be drafted, its organizations pilloried and red-baited, its idealism shattered, its mentality turned underground.

The first smell of this new McCarthyism is already in the air, burning the nostrils and poisoning the lungs.

In October of 1965 Congress enacted a law that made the burning of a draft card punishable by five years in jail and a five-thousand-dollar fine. A few weeks later, Attorney General Katzenbach announced the Justice Department was investigating SDS. In January of 1966 the Georgia state legislature refused to seat the democratically elected Julian Bond because of his opposition to the Vietnam war. In February, Congressman Olin E. Teague of Texas introduced legislation making all anti-war protests illegal; he characterized the demonstrators as "beatnik types and pseudo-intellectuals." A few days later the Michigan state legislature adopted a resolution banning Communists from speaking on campuses in the state. On March 3rd, the Justice Department petitioned the Subversive Activities Control Board to order the Du Bois Clubs to register as a Communist-front organization. Within forty-eight hours the clubs' national headquarters was blown up, and its members beaten up on a Brooklyn street, and then arrested by police. On March 26th, anti-war marches in Oklahoma City and Boston were broken up by hooligans, and in New York, twenty thousand marchers were pelted with rotten eggs, and assailed by the *Daily News* as "dupes of the communists." On March 31st, four young draft-card burners were savagely beaten on the steps of a Boston courthouse by a mob of teen-agers, while police looked on, and newsreel photographers jostled each other for close-ups of the pummeling. On April 8th the VDC headquarters in Berkeley was bombed. On May 15th a crazed gunman killed a member of the YSA in Detroit. On June

5th, a sniper waiting in ambush shot James Meredith near Hernando, Mississippi.

The other pitfall blocking the path of the New Left is the culture's skill at amiably absorbing all manner of rebels and turning them into celebrities. To be a radical in America today is like trying to punch your way out of a cage made of marshmallow. Every thrust at the jugular draws not blood, but sweet success; every hack at the roots draws not retaliation, but fame and affluence. The culture's insatiable thirst for novelty and titillation insures LeRoi Jones television interviews, Norman Mailer million-dollar royalties, and Paul Goodman fat paychecks as a government consultant. Yesterday's underground becomes today's vaudeville and tomorrow's cliché. If the draft, super-patriots, and the Justice Department don't wreck the New Left, masscult may kill it with kindness and then deposit its carcass in the cemetery of celebrities, alongside of Baby Jane Holzer, Liberace, and Jack Kerouac.

Already there are signs that the middle class enjoys being flogged by the New Radicals, while ignoring their criticisms and ideas. Magazines like *Esquire*, *Mademoiselle*, and *Playboy* have printed glowing accounts of the New Left. Publishing houses have handed out thousands of dollars to the New Radicals for books they know will indict America root and branch—but will return a handsome profit. Government agencies like the Peace Corps and the Office of Economic Opportunity have offered several of the most gifted members of the New Left lucrative jobs.

This paradox of radical ideas creating celebrities can be an insidious process. It is hard to nurse your anger if you're getting two thousand dollars to spill it out on national television. And it is hard to think creatively, or to organize effectively, if you are deluged with a stream of speaking engagements, interviews, and symposia. The danger of becoming performers subsidized to goose a decadent middle class is a real one for the New Left.

Directly toward these twin pitfalls—the escalating war in Vietnam and an endlessly absorptive culture—the New Radicals will march, just as they marched into Mississippi, Sproul Hall, and the urban slums of the North. They will continue to challenge the gods because they are cursed with the passion of Ahab and the innocence of Billy Budd. And because no one else is doing the marching.

The New Radicalism began with a request for a cup of coffee. In six years it has become a new way of looking at the world and a vision of a new kind of politics. It has given a whole generation what William James called "the moral equivalent of war."

To demand any more of this generation is to deny the responsibility of the last one—and the possibility of the next.

A graduate of Hunter College in 1961, Jack Newfield worked for the Students for Democratic Society at the time of its founding. He has been editor of a Manhattan community weekly and a reporter on the *New York Post,* and is presently assistant editor of *The Village Voice.* His articles have appeared in *The Nation* and *Commonweal.* This is his first book.

About the Author